MW01633319

www.kirkinstitute.org

Published by Life^n Books, LLC

Published 2012
ISBN: 978-1-937033-13-2

Unless otherwise indicated, all Scripture quotations in this publication are from the HOLY BIBLE, NEW AMERICAN STANDARD® . NASB®.

Cover design and layout by: Jeremy Goad. Printed in the United States of America.

For more information:

Life^n Books, LLC
James Van Eerden, Chief Editor
420 Hilton, Suite 100
Stokesdale, North Carolina 27357

www.life-n.com

TO SUFFER WELL

Discovering Hope by Understanding God's Purposes for Suffering

By Dr. Craig D. Childs, Sr.

What Others are Saying About *To Suffer Well*

I commend Craig's and Jaime's authentic story and teaching to all who have suffered – or will. The expensive lessons garnered from the sufferings surrounding their two precious sons make this book especially credible and valuable.... I will not discard my reading notes. They describe a gracious Providence, answer some of my own questions and better prepare me for the rest of the journey.

Dr. Arthur Evans Gay
Past President, The National Association of Evangelicals
Past President, World Relief Corporation

What a helpful book on suffering! I have read a lot of books on suffering but none do the comprehensive job which Craig Childs has done here.... Every Christian needs to study this book for himself, his family, and to help others. Believe me, this is a RARE opportunity – and the significance of this statement will come alive before you complete the book!

Dr. Frank M. Barker, Jr.
Pastor Emeritus, Briarwood Presbyterian Church

Suffering is universal. But suffering well is not. *To Suffer Well* is a quick read that is well written by a transparent sufferer and personal friend, Craig Childs. It is a crisp, insightful and timeless lifeline for a hurting person in a broken world.

Richard Van Eerden
Entrepreneur, Philanthropist,
Grandfather to 30 Grandkids

This book allows the reader to journey through lessons Craig has preached as a pastor and lived as a Christian. Its pages contain a wealth of wisdom that point the reader away from focusing on the storms of life – helping us instead to gaze at the One who is sovereign over all of the storms. You will be challenged to view the hardships of life through the lens of hope in a loving God.

Rev. David Russell
Executive Director
Campus Outreach Washington, DC

As I read *To Suffer Well*, I was both moved and challenged by it and began immediately to think of people to whom I would recommend it. When I read of Craig's anguish in the deepest parts of his soul which he had never known even existed, I wept as I felt for the first time that I was reading words which expressed my own soul's anguish in so much of my own suffering. To hear them expressed so plainly and yet with such hope is what we all need. I think it would be a great resource for a small group study. I give it 5 stars.

Shirley Humphrey
Reader from Moody, Alabama

To Suffer Well makes profound truths simple enough for any age. Once I began reading it, I could not put it down. I think it would make a great book for a small group study where folks could open up and truly share their suffering.

Mary Beth Walker
Reader from Birmingham, Alabama

I just finished *To Suffer Well.* I could not put it down. This book is great! I will recommend it to our church – it will make a great small group bible study.

Toni Hill
Reader from Panama City, Florida

As we read *To Suffer Well*, our hearts resonated with so much of what was said. We, too, have seen in our sufferings how the Lord was growing us and how He was with us every step of the way. You will appreciate the author's transparency as he describes his journey. We were blessed to read this book, and we know others will be blessed as well.

Ron & Sharye Norton
Reader from Greensboro, North Carolina

Good theology is essential if we
are going to suffer well.
It will help us persevere during our trials,
and it will give us hope.[1]

Dustin Shramek

And hope does not disappoint...

Romans 5:5a

If I hope in anything or anyone less than
one who has power over death,
I am doomed to final disappointment.
Suffering will drive me to hopelessness.
What character I have will disintegrate.

It is the hope of Christ that makes it
possible for us to persevere in times
of tribulation and distress. We have
an anchor for our souls that rests
in the One who has gone before us
and conquered.[2]

R.C. Sproul

TABLE OF CONTENTS

Publisher's Preface

As fellow travelers through life, we share the experience of asking questions and seeking answers in our lives. So it has been, so it will be.

That observation may seem quite obvious. But what is less obvious to some of us is that as we look back to the past and look forward to the future, it is striking how many of the questions asked and answers sought are the same for us as they were for those who journeyed before us. Mortimer Adler famously called this continuing question-and-answer pursuit "The Great Conversation."

Few questions have been more central in The Great Conversation than those relating to human suffering. Suffering troubles our minds and brings angst to our souls. Of course, the first line of trouble is why suffering exists at all. The second line of trouble is what we do with it. Ironically, much of what we do with suffering circles us back around to the question of why suffering exists in the first place.

C.S. Lewis observed that suffering is "God's megaphone to rouse a deaf world." That is true. But there are more purposes for suffering than that, as Dr. Childs observes; and if we do not understand the various aspects of God's purposes in our suffering, we will be prone to react poorly to it when it comes to us. And it will come to us.

That is the main point of this theologically rich yet concise Life^{n} reader, *To Suffer Well.* By explaining through his "5D" paradigm God's reasons for human suffering, in the context of classic Christian theology, the author shows us why and how to be hopeful in the midst of hard times and brokenness.

This is not a theoretical book. It is intensely practical. It is practical because Dr. Childs has experienced as much suffering as any man I know and, by God's grace, become the better through it. But it is also because he is more than a theologian – he is a Pastor. He reminds me of the description of the ancient road referenced by J.I. Packer in the introduction to his book *Knowing God.* Packer uses that picture to describe two kinds of theologians: those who sit up in the balcony and observe, and those who get down from the balcony and journey with the other travelers.

Dr. Childs is a "traveler theologian," and I think you will be thankful for that as you read through this important little book.

Enjoy the journey.

Jim Van Eerden
Life^{n} Books
Magnalia Forest, North Carolina

PART I

Some Preliminaries About Suffering

I have exalted one chosen out of the people.

Psalm 89:19

Christ was also chosen out of the people that He might know our wants and sympathize with us. "He was tempted in all points like as we are, yet without sin." In all our sorrows we have His sympathy.

Temptation, pain, disappointment, weakness, weariness, poverty – He knows them all, for He has felt all. Remember this, Christian, and let it comfort thee. However difficult and painful thy road, it is marked by the footsteps of thy Savior, and even when thou reachest the dark valley of the shadow of death, and the deep waters of the swelling Jordan, thou wilt find His footprints there.

In all places whithersoever we go, He has been our forerunner; each burden we have to carry, has once been laid on the shoulders of Immanuel.

C.H. Spurgeon

Charles Spurgeon
Morning by Morning

CHAPTER ONE

My Familiarity with Suffering

God is great. God is good. It's sung as a hymn and taught to children as a prayer. But we're not always sure we believe it! Why? Because of suffering.
Stuart Briscoe

Shall we indeed accept good from God and not accept adversity? In all this Job did not sin with his lips.
Job 2: 10

In my wife's home church in the 1980's, there arose a conflict surrounding a teacher who was approved to teach a mid-week class on the subject of marriage. People were in a stir. I remember one member in her sixties who complained passionately. This was her complaint: how in the world could the Elders approve a man to teach a discipleship class on marriage when that teacher had never been married himself?

While it was certainly true that the teacher could study the biblical precepts of marriage and communicate those principles to the class, no one in the class would be interested in hearing them. Why? It is because the teacher had never lived them. It is one thing to discover a biblical truth about marriage and believe it in the abstract. It is quite another thing to have sought to live that truth out in the sometimes less than perfect context of marital bliss.

It is my personal opinion that we do not have to experience everything in life in order to appreciate certain truths of our existence. For example, I do not have to be hit by a Mack truck in order to teach my children not to step out onto a busy highway. However, I am probably in agreement with my mother-in-law at this point. I do not think that I would be very excited about a teacher who had never experienced the challenges of being married to teach me how to address my issues in my marriage.

It is my suspicion that the exact same dynamic also applies to this subject of suffering. If I were you, I would be asking myself this question: Who is this Childs guy and why does he think he has something to teach me about suffering? Does this self-appointed "expert" have any experience with any deep suffering himself? I believe those to be valid questions. For that reason, I would like to share with you some of my familiarity with suffering.

Strike One: The Normal Suffering of a Normal Life

My wife (Jaime) and I have had the normal brand of suffering which comes with an average life in America today. I came from a broken home which carries with it the typical amount of anguish and scarring. We both have lost beloved pets and wondered why we sobbed so intensely over an animal. We have already buried all of our grandparents and three of our four parents.

We have both had our quota of ordinary disappointments. There were social clubs which we were not good enough for, vocational set-backs which wounded our hearts, rejections by those whom we had counted among our "friends," and so on.

Of course, there was all of that normal teenager suffering – which was real suffering then even though we look back on it now with a little different perspective.

We have some health sufferings as well. Nothing exotic, but suffering nonetheless. Jaime has a non-fatal brain tumor which requires constant medication and review. I experienced the joy of exploded Achilles tendon surgery (twice in a row), and I walk with a slight limp today. My neck surgery did not go well, so I have a constant neck "crick" pain which runs every day into my arms and fingers.

I could go on, but you undoubtedly will recognize that there is nothing extraordinary here. But you know, even the non-exotic sufferings of life can take its toll. And in the moment of that ordinary suffering, it is sometimes just as real and just as painful as the exotic versions.

Strike Two: A "Handicapped" Child

No one expects their child to be handicapped, as disabilities were labeled in my days as a young parent. Our first child, Craig Jr, was born ten weeks premature in 1975. During his birth, he was deprived of oxygen for a period of time due to abnormal tearing in the placenta. We observed that he seemed delayed in the normal sequence of infancy development, but it was not until he was 18 months old that he was diagnosed with cerebral palsy.

We were told the effect of his handicap was an uncertain factor – only time would tell. We were told that we needed to prepare for the worst. He might never walk, never talk, never control his bodily functions, or never even recognize us as his mother and father.

We were devastated! I remember lying on the floor for eight hours the next day unable to pick my head off of the carpet. No, I was not hung-over. I was swallowed up by grief. This was a deep despair over the death of dreams and hopes.

The world of a handicapped child is not the same world as a non-handicapped child. Three days a week are spent in therapy – some of which is not pleasant for the child. Sometimes he pleads with you not to take him back.

Craig did walk, but not on time. I will never forget my son's face when he noticed for the first time that his little sister, Laura, could walk and he couldn't. We were outside in the front yard at Fort Benning, Georgia. Laura was twenty months younger than Craig. She began to walk at about the normal time for walking, around the one-year-old time frame. Craig would be almost three years old before he would walk. What I saw on my young son's face that day was a fundamental reckoning that something was terribly wrong . . . with him! I went inside and locked the door of the bathroom and just cried and cried.

Then there was that little incident in the seminary apartment complex when Craig and eight other children were playing on the lawn together. Suddenly, one child said, "Let's go to the playground and play." Like a herd of elephants, they were up on their feet and dashing away at light speed to see who could win the 100 yard race to the swings. Left behind in the dust was the six-year-old with plastic casts on his legs, crying and calling out after the other children, "Wait, wait on me, I can't run and I can't get up the hill. Don't leave me." This time I stepped out the backdoor, sat down on a lawn chair, put my face in my hands and just sobbed.

So many dreams died that day in the doctor's office. Craig would be the batboy, not the shortstop. He might watch me wrestle, but he would never step on the mat and grapple himself.

And then there were the surgeries. When he was eight, they cut six muscle groups on each leg. Oh, he cried so hard because of the pain. In his mid- teens, they cut his main leg bones into two pieces and then rotated them. He lost an entire summer wearing hip casts; he only got out rarely in a wheelchair.

Well, I could tell you more of the heartache of the parents of a handicapped child. There is an endless supply of stories. My wife's perspective on those times would probably be even more saddening than my version.

However, there is good news in this tale. The Lord was gracious to us beyond measure. Craig's mind was not affected by the cerebral palsy. In fact, he was (and is) an actual genius – high school valedictorian, state champion short-story writer, champion speaker, National Merit Finalist, etc. He was and is a seventh wonder of the world (at least, to us!).

The nugget of sadness which remains with us as his parents is the knowledge that he has a handicap which the Lord has apparently designed to follow him all the days of his life. He will never run and win a race. He will walk with a cane into his children's kindergarten graduations. He will stumble on uneven ground even before we, his parents, begin to lose our balance in the senior citizen home.

For our money, having to traverse through the world of a handicapped child was more than enough suffering for our lifetime.

However, apparently, the King of the Universe did not agree with us.

Strike Three: The Death of a Child

While all suffering is painful and full of struggle, grief (as a subset of all types of suffering) often takes the heartache to an exponential level of anguish.

Clete was our fourth and youngest child. He died tragically at the age of sixteen.

I do not know how to explain to the readers of this book what it feels like to lose a child. Maybe all that I can do is to share with you an excerpt from my first book, a book on biblical parenting titled *A Guide for Biblical Parenting – for Curtain Climbers and Cookie Crumblers* (2010).

"Clete came 361 days after Alie. Neither Clete nor Alie ever remembered a day when they did not have each other at their side. They were "Irish twins". They lived and loved together. On 17 November 2005, we lost Clete when a driver swerved into his lane and hit the car he was driving-head on. He was 16 ½ years old.

There is no way to describe to you the life of our precious son Clete. Clete shared with his siblings a passionate and compassionate excitement for life. There may have never been another sixteen year old boy who was such a balance of both passion and compassion.

He was a fierce competitor on the soccer field, on the basketball court, watching Alabama football, in the debate competitions, in general discussion, in chess competitions, etc. Yet, his competitive spirit always, always, always was tempered with his high godly conscience. Like his sisters, he was a champion of the underdog and the very first friend to a lonely soul. He was one of those "once-in-a-century" personas who had indescribable ministries to people of all ages: there were three- year olds in the nursery for whom he cared for two years – they idolized him; there were elementary students who wept uncontrollably at his funeral because he was the high school student who had reached out to them when they first started school; there were middle-aged adults who wept because they felt they had lost their best friend; adults in their fifties and sixties joined our church because of Clete's outreach into their lives.

Clete was conquered by Christ at the age of eight. He never wavered in his passionate pursuit of God and His

Kingdom. He was one of the most on fire godly Christian teenage young men I have ever known. When the Lord determined to take my son to His eternal home of glory, the Kingdom of God lost one of its most powerful warriors here on earth.

On a very personal note, when we lost Clete, I lost one of my best friends. While I was his father and his authority – and not his "bud"- we shared an uncommon friendship. He was my hunting buddy, my fishing partner, my comrade in golf misadventures, my prayer partner, and my ministry's greatest cheerleader. He was more like me than any other person who has ever lived; he is the only person whom I have ever known for whom I was his unconditional hero. I miss my son terribly."

One of my most precious possessions in life today is the note which Clete wrote and gave to me on Valentine's Day 2005. Clete was almost sixteen years old at the time. He wrote:

> I don't know where to start…I don't know how to thank you for all you have done. It's the simple things in life that make one feel special, and it's the simple things in life that make me know I am loved. You may be the busiest man I know, but you always have time for me. Every game, every phone call to the church, every hunting mishap, every time I have needed you, you have been there for me. I have never felt neglected by you, but even more so, I have always felt your love. You *always* tell me that you love me; you always say, "I don't know if I have told you lately,

that I love you." Every time you tell me this, it never loses its meaning. Every night I hug and kiss you, and I would never give that up.

You have always been my source for comfort and safety. You have never let me down. A particular story comes to mind when I think of your comfort and safety. You took the whole family to Ireland, and one night I somehow managed to slam my fingers in the door. I cannot remember why, but that night I was furious at you; but still when the door slammed I called out your name. It surprised me at that time that I called your name; not because I should have called anyone else's name, but because I did not cuss, scream, or yell, but I only uttered your name. At that point I realized that no matter what I did or no matter how bad I messed up, I would always call your name.

The greatest thing you have given me is a relationship with Christ, but not only that, you have showed me how to live a Godly life, and for that I will be forever grateful. You have shown me how to honor God and to truly love the Lord our God with all my heart, soul, and mind. You have shown me patience, justice, temperance, courage, fortitude, and above all love, you have shown me these virtues in your life as a husband, father, mentor, and Christian. For this example you have shown me, I am forever grateful.

"I have no answer to give, but thanks, and thanks."- *Shakespeare*

I miss my son. It has been six years, and the taste of anguish still lingers in my heart.

You May Have Suffered More

There are no winners in an "*I have suffered more than you*" contest. There are only losers. My suspicion is that many of the readers of this book may have experienced much deeper suffering than Jaime and I have tasted.

In the fall of 2011, a couple visited the Kirk (the church where I pastor in Greensboro, North Carolina). In a subsequent e-mail communication, the father told me that his wife and he had two handicapped sons both who died in their teens – one to a sickness and one to a tragic choking event. I wept when I read his e-mail. Our life-suffering has not even been in the same league as their life-suffering.

The point is not to say that our suffering has been as bad as yours. The point is to say that we are familiar with the agony of human calamity, and we have some empathy with those of you who are up to your ears in suffering now. We understand how it feels to be looking for some relief, some comfort, some answers, some clarity, or some hope.

Stephen Saint, the son of one of the five missionaries who were slaughtered by the Waodani jungle tribesmen, agrees with this core point of this chapter as he recounts a life story:

> *I do know this:* ***sufferers want to be ministered to by people who have suffered.***

When I was a teenager, I knew a family whose son was terrible burned when he ran into a car and the gas tank on his motorcycle exploded. In the hospital burn unit he begged his mother to just let him die. She responded by inviting friends to cheer him up, but he refused to see anyone. Finally one day there was a knock on his hospital room door. When his mother opened the door there was a stranger with hideous scars all over his face and arms standing there.

The mother slammed the door, hoping her son hadn't seen the man. But he had, and insisted that his mother let the man in. His mother resisted, thinking the sight would further discourage her son. Instead of discouraging the boy, however, that man convinced the boy that there was reason to live.

People who suffer want people who have suffered to tell them there is hope.[3]

My friends, like many of you, we know a little something about suffering. We are here to tell you that there is hope in our sufferings – and hope leads to God's peace!

CHAPTER TWO
Lessons Learned from our Suffering

Our War: To follow the Warrior King, to storm the gates of hell, and to drive back the influence of darkness in ourselves, our homes, our workplaces, our community, our culture, our country, and our world.
The Kirk, Church Vision Statement

Blessed be the Lord, my rock, Who trains my hands for war, and my fingers for battle.
Psalm 144:1

Three Strikes and You're Out (?)

Dr. Childs, you told us about your three strikes of suffering. In our experience, three strikes and you are out of the game.

Not always. Not in three-year-old T ball. Not in the Kingdom of God. Not in the "War of Wars".

While I hope that this book may shed some light on why our family's suffering did not put us "out" of the ballgame, I want you to know up front that our journey of suffering has left both Jaime and me with some life-long effects. Particularly, I would like to share with you some specific lessons which suffering has taught me personally.

First, familiarity with suffering has taught me a much deeper sense of gratitude.

One of my great weaknesses as a human being is that I am loathe to need and depend upon others. I sometimes operate as an island. Thus, I have been slow to embrace deep intimacy with others and correspondingly to feel rich thankfulness toward others. Suffering has changed that – to some degree. One of the fruits of our pilgrimage of suffering is that I have seen some of the bankruptcy of my "island living". In my desperateness, I have come to be very appreciative of those who have chosen to go with me into the "Valley of the Shadow" times of my life.

I am thankful for my Captain – the King of Kings

When I was a middle school student living on a military base in Spain in the mid-sixties, there was no English-speaking TV. My only entertainment in the home was my parent's stereo. Since "rock and roll" had not gotten to Spain yet (except, of course, Elvis), I was pretty much limited to listening to my parents "Country and Western" music. It was not my favorite.

There was one song, however, which captured my fancy – even today, I can remember the refrain sung by the song's "preacher" who was facing some hard times:

You got to walk that lonesome valley
You got to walk it by yourself
Nobody else can walk it for you
You've got to walk it by yourself

While I loved the song, the theology is wrong. We do not walk it by ourselves: at least, not if we are believers.

I want to praise my Lord and Savior Jesus Christ for walking through the "Valley of the Shadow" with me as my life took its downward turns into seasons of suffering. Like the author of the well-known "Footprints" poem, there have been many segments of my life in which only one set of footprints (His) could be seen trekking through the wilderness of my journey. I sometimes felt like one of the Desert Fathers in church history – wrestling with God in my aloneness.

My wife, Jaime, and I have known some real suffering. We are card-carrying members of the Society of the Suffering Ones. We have cried a river of tears. We have been furious with God. We have screamed at Him. We have questioned His integrity. Under our breath, we may have cursed the Almighty.

How did God respond? He picked us up while we were kicking and screaming and carried us through the dark times. He held us close. He wiped away our tears. He put His arms around us and told us how much He loved us. He reminded us of Who He is, who we are, and Whose we are. And along the way, He taught us some things about suffering.

I am thankful for my wife, Jaime Garner Childs

Although I did not really officially "meet" Jaime until college, I do have a "first memory" of her from the halls of our high school. I remember seeing her in a 1968 miniskirt and thinking to myself: "wow, what great looking legs" (you know, with the godly admiration of a teenage boy). Little did I know at that time that this young slim beautiful fifteen-year girl would become my partner in all things which would ultimately matter in my life.

Jaime is the one who has put up with me for almost four decades (wed in 1973) and has been my lifelong partner. Her commitment to be my wife has been for better or for worse, for richer or for poorer (mostly poor), and in sickness and in health. Our life together has had more than its fair share of calamity. We have faced our sufferings together. We have cried together (although I usually tried to hide it). We have been confused together. We have anguished together. We have walked through the Valley of the Shadow together. I could not ask for a more faithful partner.

I believe that the latest statistics which I have seen indicate that 80% of the couples who experience the death of a child in a manner similar to how we lost Clete, end up in divorce, depression, or worse. With all confidence, I can say that I am absolutely certain that if Jaime had not been the woman of character that she is, neither our marriage nor my sanity would have survived the wilderness experience of losing our beloved Clete.

My Lord and Savior Jesus Christ was unbelievably gracious to me the day that He gave me the special gift of Jaime Garner to be my wife. You realize, of course, that I had no idea on that day what a blessing she would be for me. Just so that you can understand my unbelievable shallowness, I thought I was marrying her just because she had great looking legs.

I am thankful for "bad weather" friends

Like the Prodigal Son, we may have many 'friends' when times are good – we call them our "fair weather friends." But, you really know who your friends are when the "bad weather" rolls in. I am particularly thankful for a handful of close friends who have walked with me through a recent "Valley of the Shadow" season in my calling as a Pastor.

There is the maverick motorcycle mob, a multitude of misfits, and my own children (and their spouses) who have walked this valley with me. Several of these friends serve on the Advisory Board of the Kirk Institute. Many of them belong to the Kirk, our family of families which walks together in daily and weekly fellowship from this life toward the next.

These men and women have encouraged me to believe that I am not yet all washed up and have inspired me to write out some of the things which I have been teaching in discipleship groups for thirty years now.

Some of those friends have even helped me edit this book, and have helped me to traverse my way through the darkness and to see God's hand in leading me into a new season of ministry. My hunting buddies who share my love for the Lord's outdoors have been dear to me. (It is often at weird times on those outings that some of the most encouraging and helpful things get shared.)

Thank you, Lord, for giving me "bad weather" friends who have jumped into the pit with me and have fanned the flames of hope and possibilities for me and who are willing to hold me accountable to "finish strong" in this fourth quarter of life ministry for You.

Second, familiarity with suffering has taught me perspective

Besides giving me a great appreciation for those who are willing to walk with me through the wilderness experiences of my life, the Lord has used my familiarity with suffering to help me gain a truer perspective on life here upon this earth.

Perspective is everything

In my opinion, gaining a perspective on a matter is everything. I am reminded of an old "feudal times" story of a stranger passing a number of men doing masonry work on large stones.

When he passed the first man, he noticed that the man seemed depressed, discouraged, and at the end of his rope. The stranger asked the first man: "What are you doing?" With a grumble and a glare, the first worker responded, "I'm pounding on these stupid stones in this pile of never-ending stones."

When the stranger approached the second worker, the stranger noticed a much different demeanor. This worker, while appearing tired and weary, was busy at work with an appearance of confidence and satisfaction. As the worker checked and rechecked his work, the stranger could sense a man who took pride in his accomplishments. He asked this second worker, "What are you doing?" With a weary smile, the second worker replied, "Why, I'm building a wall, and it is going to be straight and strong."

However, when the stranger approached a third worker, he was caught off guard with the unusual peppiness which this mason seemed to have. While clearly working harder than both of the previous workers, this third worker appeared to do his work with effortless endeavor. There was a skip in his step. He was whistling a tune. There was a huge smile on his face. Curious concerning this odd behavior, the stranger asked this worker the same question: "What are you doing?" With an absolute glow of excitement on his face, this third worker exclaimed passionately, "Haven't you heard, we are building a Cathedral for the Lord."

What made the difference in the attitude of the three workers? The answer: *Perspective.*

Perspective is the lens of life by which we understand and integrate our life experiences into a broader understanding of a grander tapestry of purpose. When it comes to suffering, perspective is everything.

My perspective prior to suffering: safe, warm, & comfortable

There is no way to make this sound pretty. Before the Lord took me down the dirt road of suffering, life was all about me. In fact, salvation was all about me.

What I mean is that almost everything in my relationship with my Lord and Savior revolved around the question of how the Lord might make my life better. If I walked with Him and if I served Him, then He would insure that my life would be good – and by that I understood that He would protect me from mishap, shield me from pain, keep my family safe, make me successful in my vocational pursuits, give me good health, and generally handle all of my problems. C.S. Lewis described it like this:

> *What would really satisfy us would be a God who said of anything we happened to like doing, "What does it matter so long as they are contented?" We want, in fact, not so much a Father in Heaven as a grandfather in heaven– a senile benevolence who, as they say, "liked to see young people enjoying themselves," and whose plan for the universe was simply that it might be truly said at the end of each day, "a good time was had by all." Not many people, I admit, would formulate a theology in precisely those terms; but a conception not very different lurks at the back of many minds. I do not claim to be an exception…*[4]

In other words, my relationship with the Lord was all about Him keeping me safe, warm, and comfortable – it was all about Him making my life a "good time".

It sounds quite shallow doesn't it? Maybe you are there. Well, it doesn't take much suffering at all to upset that applecart.

My perspective after suffering: The War of Wars

It did not happen all at once. Little by little, the Lord changed my perspective on the essence of life here on this planet. I have to come to understand that it really is not all about me. Rather, it is all about Him.

You see, there is a King. And this King has a reign. It is called the Kingdom of Light. The purpose of this Kingdom of Light is to deliver captives from the bondage of the darkness of this world and to bring them into His orbit. The King shines His Light into the darkness and beckons to the slaves of the darkness. "This way to life!", He proclaims to the captives. The King wants to do this because He is the essence of love.

The darkness is not too keen on giving up its dominion. Darkness hates the Light. Darkness fights against the work of the King. Enmity ensues. Thus, there exists this spiritual warfare which we members of the Kirk (the church) Universal often refer to as the "War of Wars."

Unfortunately, suffering is part and parcel of this War of Wars.

Those of us who know Christ have a Warrior King Who is leading us into spiritual warfare against these forces of darkness. Although sometimes it may look like darkness is winning a skirmish or two, we are absolutely certain that our Captain knows what He is doing, and we know how this War is going to end (we have seen the end of the Book). He wins! We win!

> *But until then, we fight!*
> *Blessed be the Lord, my rock*
> *Who trains my hands for war*
> *And my fingers for battle (Psalm 144:1)*

Kingdom life is not a Rose Garden; it is a battlefield. It is not a picnic; it is a string of skirmishes. It is not about our lives being "safe, warm, and comfortable" – it is instead about the Lord driving back the darkness in our hearts, in our homes, our workplaces, our community, our culture, our country, and our world.

You see, it is really not all about us. It never was. It is all about Him. It is about His victory over darkness.

And in this War of Wars, He chooses to use the instrument of suffering to *deliver* us from the bondage of darkness, to *discipline* us from the power of darkness in our own lives, to *develop* us for our role in the War, to *deploy* us into battle in that War, and to prepare us for our ultimate *destiny* when we will war no more.

This is the perspective which gives me hope when I experience the suffering of the Valley of the Shadow.

Third, familiarity with suffering has taught me about the great seductiveness of suffering

Over the last thirty years, I have taught this material on suffering within a broader discipleship module which was entitled "Seductions". This module contained discipleship lessons developed on a plethora of life dynamics which all tend to entice or seduce us away from an intimate walk with our Savior, Jesus Christ. Other dynamics studied in this module were anger, worry, depression, tongue-taming, pride, money, etc.

Unlike some of the more obvious assaults of darkness against our relationship with the Lord, these "seductions" are more subtle in how they lure us away from a trust and dependence upon Christ.

Most of us know of the Christian author C.S. Lewis. Although I don't agree with everything Lewis writes, it is my opinion that there have been few men as influential as Lewis in the development of Christian thought in the last century. When Clete was killed, I was given and quickly read the journal *(A Grief Observed)* which Lewis wrote in the first few months following the death of his wife. In reading this book as it described his stage of grief at that time, I was stunned by the sense which I got that this deeply thoughtful theologian was himself thrown into a season of great doubt and even disbelief.

However, as I continued to walk through the indescribable Valley of the Shadow of grief which set in not long after Clete's funeral, I tasted myself of some of the deep despair which Lewis seemed to describe in his book. To be candid, this period of suffering led me into a season of unparalleled doubt in my Christian life. Never in my 38 years as a believer had I ever doubted anything about the Lord, the Scriptures, or the Kingdom. During this season of grief, I doubted everything!

Was all of this God-stuff just made up in my mind? Had I wasted my entire adult life on the pursuit of a myth? If God was real, is He really just a cruel cad? How could a loving God do this to a child who had loved Him beyond description and to a family which had walked with Him for decades? I am not sure at all if I want to follow a God who is this unfair! Similarly, Lewis would refer to Him as a "Cosmic Sadist" during his worst time of despair.

In His unfathomable grace, God did not give me what I deserved for my heretical attitude and words. He would have been right and just to discard me as no longer usable in any form whatsoever for His purposes. Instead, He drew me back toward Him by leading me through a deep reflection upon the Lordship of Christ as evidenced by His resurrection from the dead.

As I have said from the pulpit many times, everything in our faith stands or falls on the historical truthfulness of the resurrection of Jesus. The reality of the resurrection was the theological anchor which the Lord used to keep me from crashing my boat on the rocks of disbelief. This anchor line is what He eventually used to reel me back into an even deeper trust in Him.

I tell you all of this so that you will understand why I hope this book will help believers who find themselves in the deep despair often associated with suffering. I have come to believe that it may be suffering that is the greatest of all of the seducers. It seduced me to the very edge of rejection. Even the great C.S. Lewis was seduced to the point of doubt.

My friends, do not lose heart if the suffering in your life has enticed you to the point of great despair. That is the nature of this seduction. That is why suffering can be such a powerful tool in the hands of darkness.

This is why I have written this book – to help stop the seductive slide which suffering often inflicts upon those who belong to God.

Fourth, my familiarity with suffering has led me to write this book.

Suffering is a quagmire.

Life is often hard. Our experiences of hardship are frequently confusing. It is difficult to understand why "bad" things happen to "good" people. The "Yellow Brick Road" is a lie. "Happily Ever After" is a myth. The big church is heretical when it teaches that God will bring us "Health and Wealth" if we just will have enough faith. There are more questions than answers.

The truth is that I have read a lot of books on suffering (particularly on grief) over the years. Many have been disappointments (at least to me). Some have been heresy. A few have been helpful. I am not really sure if this book has been authored because the book *needs* to be written or because I *need* to write the book. Maybe it is a combination of both.

Please note that this small book is intended only to be a "primer" on the fundamentals of suffering. That is all. It does not aim to provide:

- Answers to all of the questions which arise during suffering; but it may answer some.
- Explanations to all of the scriptural complexities which orbit the issue of suffering; but it does shed some light on the subject.
- Suggestions for all of God's sovereign purposes in ordering suffering into our lives; but it does discuss

five of His purposes for suffering (which over the years in my discipleship groups have been referred to as "The Five Ds of Suffering").

My prayer is that perhaps the Lord will use this book to help some of us to see this matter of suffering in the context of a bigger picture and a brighter light. To become fruitful warriors in the Kingdom, ultimately we must see our own suffering in the context of the broader landscape of the War of Wars –which is much bigger than our own front yard. Only then will we emerge from our experiences of suffering healthier than when we entered into the Valley of the Shadow.

CHAPTER THREE

Important Truths about Suffering

"If God were good, He would wish to make His creatures perfectly happy, and if God were almighty, He would be able to do what He wished. But the creatures are not happy. Therefore God lacks either goodness, or power, or both." This is the problem of pain, in its simplest form.[5]
C.S. Lewis

He causes His sun to rise on the evil and the good, and sends rain on the righteousness and the unrighteousness.
Matthew 5:45

There is so very much which we do not understand about suffering. There are deep burning questions on this subject which seem to defy comprehensible answers. To make matters worse, there are a handful of heretical conclusions which parade around as seemingly "self-evident" truths. Unfortunately, several of these false heresies seem to be the default positions of many who claim to be so-called experts on the subject of suffering.

However, in contrast to those heretical default positions, there are a handful of simple biblical truths which orbit around the complexities of human suffering in the scriptures. Here, we will attempt to lay out for the readers a few of those foundational preliminary principles which the Word of God teaches to us.

Heresy: You have heard it said that -- if God is good, then there can be no satisfactory explanation for the origin of suffering. Since suffering exists, God must be a Cosmic Sadist.[6]

But the truth is: Suffering is a consequence of our fallen state, not some evil nature of our God.

In the beginning, there was the Triune God – and none other. Then, He created. Then came the earth. Then came man, and then woman. In the State of Innocence, there in the original created order in the historical Garden of Eden, the best we can tell from the Word of God, there was no suffering in any aspect of life. Everything was good!

There was the Ordinance of Work (Gen. 2:15).

Apparently, there was a joy in work for Adam. There were no problems on the job. Machinery never broke down. Computers never went off line. There was no raunchy boss. No lazy employees. No office politics. Adam never rolled over, cut off the alarm, pulled the covers over his head, and asked Eve to call him in sick. He never came home after work and plopped down in the lazy boy and moaned about a hard day at the office. There was no suffering at work.

There was the Ordinance of Marriage (Gen. 2: 18-25).

It is hard for us to imagine a perfect marital intimacy. No interpersonal conflicts. No in-law tensions. No miscommunications. No arguments about sex. No battle of wills over headship and leadership in the family. No frustration concerning whose job it is to take out the trash or to put the tea on the table (a personal idiom between Jaime and myself). Can we even comprehend a marriage between one man and one woman with nothing but encouragement, edification, selfless sacrifice, joy, laughter, and (I believe) unbridled passion? There was no suffering in interpersonal human relationships, especially marriage.

There was the Ordinance of Sabbath
(Gen.2:3/ Ex. 20: 8-11).

God gave the human race the perfect balance of work and rest and reflection and worship – and (I believe) play and fun and passion. Stress from overwork did not exist. Eve was never worn out with housework. Their bodies never felt like collapsing from exhaustion. There was no suffering in the fundamental rhythm of life-work-play.

In God's original created order, Adam and Eve had a perfect environment, perfect employment, perfect relationships with others, perfect relationship with all of the animal kingdom and all of nature, perfect rhythm with the order and flow of life's dynamics, perfect bodies, perfect earth, and most importantly, a perfect intimacy with the Lord God. *In the beginning, there was no suffering!*

And then came the sneaky snake, the forbidden fruit, and the Fall of mankind!

One might ask: why would this sin by Adam and Eve in the Book of Genesis be considered so heinous that man's constitution would be shattered, suffering would enter the world, and the created order would itself begin to groan under the weight of the curse? Why did this disobedience begin the fall of dominos which would introduce anguish, pain, and calamity into our existence?

C.S. Lewis helps us understand the enormity of humanity's sin. The Lord had created man and woman to be the objects of His love, His care, His shalom. He put them in the perfect context with perfect relationships and perfect access to Him.

In response to the Creator's love and grace, the creatures, in effect, told the Sovereign to take a flying leap. They wanted to be the Captains of their own ship. They wanted "*to call their souls their own... they wanted some corner in the universe of which they could say to God, "This is our business, not yours."*"[7]

But since there was no such corner in that original created order and since the Master had created humanity with freedom to choose, He changed the constitution of their nature, their environment, their relationships, and their everything! He gave us what we demanded.

It only takes a cursory look at the curses in Genesis 3 to see that everything changed after the Fall. There is pain in parenting. There is warfare between Light and darkness. There is the marital grappling for the reins of leadership in the home. The ground now betrays man, and work has become a chore.

Even though the Lord promises that He will bring good results from these struggles (He gifts children to us, He provides for the order in the family, and He brings forth bread from our sweat and toil), nevertheless, life has now become full of trials, ordeals, fears, worries, conflicts, and death. Suffering has entered into the world:

- marital conflict (Gen. 3:16)
- disobedient and unruly children who break the hearts of their parents (Dt. 21:18)
- deep internal psychological, emotional, and spiritual struggles (Rom. 7)
- divorce
- storms of nature (Mt. 7), natural disasters, and the groaning of creation (Rom 8:22)
- disease
- death of children (2 Sam 12)
- spiritual warfare (Gen 3:15 and Eph 6:10-20)
- old age

So, who is responsible for the suffering in the world? We are – not the birds, not the elephants, and certainly not the Lord.

Adam and Eve were created with an ideal nature in the State of Innocence which had two natural abilities – the ability to perfectly please God all of the time and the ability to sin. You might ask, "Why in the world would God have created mankind with a choice between these two abilities?"

That is a great question. Have you ever seen either version of the movie "Stepford Wives"? In that movie, men replaced their human wives with identical anatomically-perfect robots. Their robot wives always said the most loving and encouraging comments imaginable. They were perfect in both the kitchen and the bedroom. The creator of these robot wives assumed that no man could possible ask for anything more than the perfect wife who would never do anything even remotely discourteous or disrespectful to the husband. The outcome, however, was something much different. The truth is that the robot wife could neither experience nor give real love. And without the choice of love, the entire relationship was a meaningless farce. Love must be a choice – and robots have no choice.

After writing this section connecting love, freedom, evil, and suffering, I ran across Peter Kreeft's book, *Making Sense Out of Suffering*, in which he repeatedly makes these exact same connections:

> The only way to guarantee a world without evil is to create us un-free....To prevent all evil, you must remove all freedom.[8]

> ...and if God had to risk justice in order to guarantee love, that is what He did...better love and injustice than no love. Making us

> robots would have guaranteed justice but at the expense of love.[9]

Why did the Sovereign Master of the universe give the first humans in the Garden a choice? It is because God is love and He desired for His creations to be able to truly feel and experience this unbelievable attribute known as unconditional love. In order for the relationship between the Lord and mankind truly to be a relationship of love, then mankind had to be creatures with a choice. They could not be simply robots programmed to tell God what He wanted to hear.

So, we made our choice!

It is the human race which is responsible for the Fall and for the suffering which entered into the world as a result of the Lapse. It is a consequence of the actions and choices of both the initial homo sapiens and their seed after them.

My goal in presenting this first truth of suffering to you is not to produce any sense of guilt. Rather, it is to help us see that all pain and suffering exists today as an unavoidable part of the fabric of the falleness of the world which we have inherited. There is no escape from suffering in this era.

Suffering will last until one of two things occur: we enter the State of Glory through our personal death or we enter the State of Glory because our Champion returns.

Either way, those of us who have come to know Jesus Christ as our Redeemer and King can look forward to an existence one day when the State of Glory leaves us with only the ability to perfectly please the Lord all of the time. All of our tears will be wiped away (Rev. 21: 1-5). There will be no more death, no more mourning, no more crying, no more pain, no more disease, no more catastrophes, no more funerals, no more broken hearts, no more conflict, no more fear, no more worry, no more dashed dreams. Bottom line, there will be no more suffering.

Until then, however, we live with the suffering of our falleness!

Heresy: You have heard it said that -- if God were all-powerful, He would stop all suffering. Since suffering does exist, then God must not really be in control of all life.

But the truth is: God is indeed Sovereign over all suffering.

I remember a women's group which I led for almost two years in the mid-eighties at our first church. One of our most interesting and heated discussions came when we tackled the Problem of Evil. At one point in the discussion, several grown women in their thirties were standing on the top of their chairs yelling and insisting that God cannot possibly be Sovereign over suffering.

I remember the real struggle when we studied in Job chapter one. Here Satan comes from roaming about on the earth (Job 1:7) looking for some poor soul to devour (1 Pet. 5:8). And lo and behold, our Lord dangles Job right in front of Satan like a fish on a hook just baiting

Satan into wanting to sift Job with pain and suffering. How could God do that? Why would God do this? Those were burning questions for those godly women.

The study of Matthew 4 (verse 1) did not help when everyone realized that it was God the Holy Spirit Who actually led the Incarnate Jesus into the very lair of Satan to undergo the sufferings of temptation. Does God really oversee and direct our contexts of suffering?

It was the study of Isaiah 45: 6-7 which left no doubt – only questions:

> *That men may know from the rising to the setting*
> *of the sun that there is no one besides Me.*
> *I am the Lord, and there is no other.*
> *The One forming light and creating darkness*
> *Causing well-being and creating calamity;*
> *I am the Lord who does all these.*

It is puzzling. How is it that our God of love can be sovereign over evil, suffering, and calamity?

We touched on this previously. In the Lord's Omnipotent Sovereignty, He originally placed humanity into a created order which empowered human beings to have a real freedom to love and trust his Creator. Since the Sovereign wished for His creation to have "real life and real love", His Omnipotence created choice and therefore the potential for calamity and suffering.

After the Fall, He then, in His Sovereignty, affords Himself the avenue of Providence whereby He works in concurrence with the "second cause" of man's will (even man's will which sometimes chooses evil) and other second causes whereby He preserves and governs His creation.

As Mark Talbot has written, "*God never does evil. Yet this is not to say that God does not create, send, permit, or even move others to do evil....*" *God never does evil, but in His absolute Sovereignty He "...ordains any evil there is. To say that God 'ordains' something is to say that He has planned and purposed and willed it from before the creation of the world – that is, from before time began.*"[10]

It still sounds somewhat confusing, doesn't it? To be candid, it is difficult for our human minds to really comprehend the paradoxical nuances of how the Lord can be sovereign over calamity, suffering, sin, and evil. All this talk of "first cause" and "second causes" is hard to grasp. What does it mean for God to ordain suffering but not be the author of it? What is the difference between the concept of God "doing evil" (which He does *not* do) and the concept of God creating calamity, sending suffering, and directing others to do evil (which God *does* do)?

While not everyone agrees that the distinction which I am about to share with you is helpful, I can tell you that it is helpful for me. I will often use a unique term to describe God's sovereignty over suffering. I will say that God "choreographs" suffering in our lives. I choose this term because I am favorably impressed by the insightful teaching of the Westminster Confession of Faith on the subject of Providence (Chapter V). Here, the Confession teaches several truths which help me understand this antinomy better.

- God is the "first cause" of all things which come to pass.
- God ordinarily causes all things which come to pass to fall out according to the nature of "second causes". He, of course, can work without or even against second causes, at His pleasure.
- God's Providence extends itself to the first Fall and all other sins of angels and men.
- God's Providence is more than bare permission; rather it is the active *bounding*, *ordering*, and *governing* of such sins, chaos, and calamity in order to bring about His holy ends.
- God is never the author or approver of sin.

For me, the concept of "choreography" best conceptualizes this role of our Heavenly Father Who actively directs, bounds, orders, and governs the sins of men and angels which are the true "authors" of the suffering in our lives. While it is the sins of men and angels which may author the dance and then dance the dance, it is Father Who choreographs the dance into the whole tapestry of the big picture.

Then in the midst of the choreography, God makes a move which darkness never saw coming. In the heart of the play, the Sovereign Himself jumps into the pit of sin, evil, and suffering with His People in order to comfort those whom He loves and to choreograph the Shadow of the Valley to produce His ultimate "good". He was in the fiery furnace with Daniel's friends (Daniel 3:25). At the Incarnation, He was Immanuel. Today His Holy Spirit indwells us, and He is with us always (Matthew 28: 20)

For me, the greatest comfort which I can experience in the times of the Valley of the Shadow is that this is a fundamental truth taught in the Scriptures. God is Sovereign! Nothing can happen to me in this fallen world unless it first passes through the hands of my Heavenly Father and is sent by Him. And when it does happen to me, the Great Lover of my Soul joins me in the pit of calamity.

When I read what Joseph said in Gen. 50:20, then I can undergo underhanded treatment at the hands of other men and women and still believe that God will cause it to bring about good results.

One of my favorite verses in all of the Bible is Romans 8:28. God is Sovereign over my suffering and He takes responsibility for ultimately insuring that all things (even my sufferings) will work together for good for me and mine. Now that verse does not say that we will always understand how God turns it out for good.

Sometimes, we can see the "Good"

Jaime and I both have seen some of the real 'good' which the Lord brought forth from Craig Jr's handicap, as an example of this. Both of us realize that our Father used this suffering to change and to alter the entire course of our family.

Prior to Craig's handicap, I believe that I was destined to be one of those fathers who pushed their children (especially the boys) to perform in the realm of athletics and academics, at the expense of the hearts of the children. I am certain that I would have become one of those obnoxious fathers who screamed at their kids and cursed at the umpires at the games.

God's Sovereign action to bestow upon our family the "Special Gift" of a handicapped child changed everything for us. It changed our priorities. It changed our processes as parents. It eventually changed our hearts toward all four of our children. It is my absolute conviction that all four of our children walk with the Lord today because of the changes which the Master made in our hearts as parents due to our struggling with the experience of a handicapped child.

Sometimes, however, we cannot see the "Good"

Six years after Clete's death, I have yet to really see the "good" in losing Clete. I am probably blinded by my own grief and pain and selfishness. It just seems to me that Clete's grand passion for Him could have already brought forth tremendous fruit for the Kingdom had the Lord left him here with us. Neither Jaime nor I see it. However, both of us are absolutely certain that our Father has already and will continue to bring about His "good" from the death of our son. (And, of course, Clete is having the time of his life!)

I can take a pretty mediocre theological stab at addressing the Problem of Evil and God's Sovereign role in our suffering (after all, I have been to seminary and isn't seminary supposed to give us all of the answers), but the truth is that there are many more questions than answers.

This is my anchor, however. My God is Sovereign over everything that happens or fails to happen to me. There are no exceptions. He is not asleep at the wheel. There are no accidents – at least not in the ultimate scheme of things.

God is in absolute control, and He has His reasons and will ultimately bring about His purposes through the means of my suffering. My guess is that the experience of our sufferings, even as a consequence of clear and present evil in the world, is used by the Lord to bring forth His purposes for His People in this fallen world.

Of course, as Ravi Zacharias reminds us, we must "remember that every worldview – not just Christianity's – must give an explanation or an answer for evil and suffering...this is not just a problem distinctive to Christianity. It will not do for the challenger just to raise the question. This problem of evil is one to which we all must offer an answer, regardless of the belief system to which we subscribe."[11]

Christianity does offer an answer. The Five Purposes for Suffering which comprise the framework for this book represent my attempt to explain what some of God's good purposes may be for me in my sufferings, and for you in yours.

Heresy: You have heard it said that if you are faithful to God, He will protect you from all suffering. He will not let bad things happen to good people.

But the truth is: Suffering comes upon the Just and the Unjust (Believers in the Lord do not get a "free pass").

I believe that there is a deep demonic heresy being taught today in certain corners of the Church in America. We can see it on television. We can read it in sermons. The heresy teaches us that if we are faithful and if we are "full of faith" in our walk with God, then God will protect us from suffering. God will provide for us "health and wealth", family peace, business blessings, and basically almost any good thing which we desire. *Walk right with God and God will treat you right!*

Most of us who have studied the Holy Scriptures know that this heresy is not new. In fact, this was the very perspective which Job's friends and advisors brought to try to help Job in his suffering. As my seminary professor explained it to me, Job's counselors came with the "Deuteronomic Assumption" (Dt. 27 and 28): if believers make good choices, God insures that blessings come upon you; if believers make wrong choices, then God insures that curses come upon you. Their message was this: *Job, since you are suffering, then you must have made wrong choices. If you had made godly choices, then you would be continuing to live the life of "health and wealth" and family blessings.*

The fundamental core of this heresy is this: the good do not die young and bad things do not happen to good people. Oh, precious followers of Christ, please believe me when I tell you that this is a lie from hell!

It is Jesus Himself who explicitly teaches us that "health and wealth" theology is false. In the Sermon on the Mount, He makes it clear that the rain falls on the just and the unjust (Mt. 5:45). I do not know how He could have made it any clearer. Because we live in a fallen world, it rains on everybody's parade.

Also in the Sermon on the Mount, this Second Person of the Godhead paints for us the picture of the two lives (see also Psalm 1 and Jeremiah 17). One house is built on the rock and one house is built on the sand. While almost everyone discerns the reality that one house stands and one house falls because of the foundation upon which they have staked everything, most of us do not see at first this additional fundamental premise: *the storm comes upon both houses.* The believer who has built his life upon the rock of the gospel does not get a pass from the storm.

I am certain that some of you are thinking this: No, Dr. Childs, you are not correct. My pastor assures me that if I live right and trust the Lord enough, then God will protect me and mine.

You know, the reason that this heresy finds such fertile ground in our souls is because we deeply yearn for the life of the Garden of Eden. We think that the "yellow brick road" and the "happily-ever-after" promises are still intended for us here on earth. Like you, I really yearn for the heresy to be true.

However, the heresy is false. *In The Pilgrim's Progress,* John Bunyan tells us that even Worldly Wiseman could recognize that the life of Christian would be fraught with some hardship and difficulty.

> *"Before long, he met another traveler – Worldly Wiseman, from the Town of Worldly Wisdom, near the City of Destruction.*
>
> *'Where are you going, weary traveller?' Worldly Wiseman greeted Christian.*
>
> *'To the gate – to be freed from my burden,' was the reply.*
>
> *'Who told you to go this way?'*
>
> *'Evangelist.'*
>
> *'I might have known!' snorted Worldly Wiseman. 'This is a dangerous route. You have already encountered the Slough of Despond; if you continue on this road, you will face weariness and pain, dragons and darkness, death and many other dangers."*[12]

What the Scriptures Teach

Principle: Sometimes, God chooses to protect believers from certain sufferings.

An example of this is the Lord protecting His People from the tenth plague (the death of the first-born child) which God used to deliver Israel from Pharaoh (Ex. 11). However, God has nowhere promised that He will always choose to protect us from suffering.

Principle: Often, God orchestrates that believers go through the Valley of the Shadow of suffering.

- Abel brought the righteous offering (Gen. 4), and he was murdered by his brother because of it.
- Noah was a righteous man (Gen. 6: 8-9). Yet, his world was turned upside down by the disaster of the flood.
- The Apostle Paul undergoes a life of regular suffering (jail, beatings, rejections, shipwrecks, and more) because of his mission for Christ. (2 Cor 11: 24ff)
- The author of Hebrews 11: 36-40 delineates a plethora of suffering for the heroes of faith.
- History tells us that ten of the disciples died horrible deaths which ended their lives of ministry for Christ.
- The early Christians were tortured and killed in the persecutions of Rome.

Principle: Here is what God has promised. He will go with us through the suffering.

He is Immanuel (Mt.1:23). He will walk with us through the Valley of the Shadow (Ps. 23). He will never leave us. He will be with us always (Mt. 28:20). Even when we cannot sense Him in our times of horror, He is there – picking us up and carrying us when we are done for.

My dear friends, Scripture does not teach that we get a pass on suffering because we are in His family. We, too, must live in the fallen world. Nowhere does our Heavenly Father promise us a Rose Garden.

Craig Jr. has Cerebral Palsy and will probably walk with a cane and a limp all of his life. Clete never calls me anymore on Father's Day because there are no phones in heaven. My grandfather's old age spots have somehow begun to appear on my hands. For no good reason I know of, a disk in my neck decided to bulge when I made a play at second base which I had made hundreds of times before. The pain lingers even after the surgery. And then there was that basketball Achilles tendon rupture which never healed right, even after the second surgery.

The heresy is a lie. Suffering is part of our world. Yet, Jesus never fails to show up in the midst of our suffering. He understands the stress which suffering puts on our faith. He sympathizes with both our weaknesses and our pain. This is why He represents us as our High Priest (Heb. 4:15). The cross and the resurrection are our assurance that the Lord will walk us through the Valley of the Shadow. There will be light at the end of the tunnel, even if we are not able to understand it.

Heresy: You have heard it said that since suffering is so unfair and so painful, then any response on our part, no matter how violent or how vile, is both understandable and justifiable.

But the truth is: Our response to suffering is both important and controllable. (Our pain does not give us a "blank check" to respond and to vent as we wish).

The bulk of the remainder of this book is aimed at unfolding the "Five Purposes for Suffering".

Toward the end of this primer on suffering, I will address the importance of considering our response to God's sanctifying work in our hearts which He seeks to accomplish in us through the medium of earthly suffering.

We can discover in Scripture and in our own experiences that there are a number of unbecoming responses to our sufferings: responses like bitterness, complaining, anger, sourness, blame-shifting, impatience, and revenge.

We can also discover from the Word of God a number of godly responses to suffering:

- Job praises God for his suffering (Job 1:20-22)
- The Apostles rejoice over their sufferings (Acts 5:40-41)
- Stephen forgives (Acts 7: 59-60)
- Paul gets perspective (Romans 8:18)

In Chapter 9 of this book, I will share a simple acrostic (R-A-R-E) response to sufferings which has helped me in my walk with Him. In my humble opinion, our response to suffering is the one key element of our suffering which we can influence. I believe that it both aids in our sanctification process and gives us peace in the midst of the storms. I am convinced that our response to our sufferings is critically important.

PART II

Some Purposes for Suffering

The things which are not seen.
2 Corinthians 4:18

In our Christian pilgrimage it is well, for the most part, to be looking forward. Forward lies the crown, and onward is the goal. Whether it be for hope, for joy, for consolation, or for the inspiring of our love, the future must, after all, be the grand object of the eye of faith.

Looking into the future we see sin cast out, the body of sin and death destroyed, the soul made perfect, and fit to be a partaker of the inheritance of the saints in light. Looking further yet, the believer's enlightened eye can see death's river passed, the gloomy stream forded, and the hills of light attained on which standeth the celestial city; he seeth himself enter within the pearly gates, hailed as more than conqueror, crowned by the hand of Christ, embraced in the arms of Jesus, glorified with Him, and made to sit together with Him on His throne, even as He has overcome and has sat down with the Father on His throne.

The thought of this future may well relieve the darkness of the past and the gloom of the present. The joys of heaven will surely compensate for the sorrows of earth.

Hush, my fears! This world is but a narrow span, and thou shalt soon have passed it. Hush, hush, my doubts! Death is but a narrow stream, and thou shalt soon have forded it. Time, how short– eternity, how long!. Death, how brief– immortality, how endless! Methinks I even now eat of Eshcol's clusters, and sip of the well which is within the gate. The road is so, so short! I shall soon be there.

C.H. Spurgeon

Charles Spurgeon
Morning by Morning

CHAPTER FOUR

The First Purpose for Suffering: Deliverance

Calamity is good in life; it took calamity to bring me to the Lord.
Don Dickinson

And he was longing to fill his stomach with the pods that the swine were eating, and no one was giving anything to him. But when he came to his senses, he said, "How many of my father's hired men have more than enough bread, but I am dying here with hunger! I will get up and go to my father, and will say to him, 'Father, I have sinned against heaven, and in your sight.'"
Luke 15: 16-18

As we study the Word of God, one can discover that one of the reasons that the Lord God choreographs suffering into the lives of humans is "Deliverance". What is meant here is that God ordains suffering for some in order to deliver them from the bondage of the kingdom of darkness and to usher those persons into the Kingdom of Light.

The central thrust of this suffering seems to be to bring the targeted person to the end of himself. The suffering appears to be aimed at producing brokenness in the soul of the person. This suffering, like a scalpel, seeks to strip away from the person the facade of self-control, the myth of self-reliance, the hoax of self-sufficiency, and the heresy of self-righteousness.

For many persons, it is only when we have been slaughtered by suffering that we become open to seeing our need for our Creator and King. Only when we see ourselves as helpless, do we see our need for the Redeemer. Only when we see ourselves as the prideful and arrogant creatures which we really are, can we see our need to become a beloved child of the Father.

Consider the Prodigal Son

While I realize that there may be some commentators who believe that the Parable of the Prodigal Son is about the discipline of a believer who is already part of the Family and not the deliverance of a non-believer, it is my conviction that grammatical contextual exegisis leads to the certain conclusion that this parable is picturing the conversion of a non-believer. If you look closely at Luke 15, you will see that it is a grouping of three "lost" parables: a lost sheep, a lost coin, and finally a lost son.

In Luke 15, Jesus teaches us so clearly in the Parable of the Prodigal son. Here was an arrogant self-centered son who felt he had no need for the father or the family. He could make it on his own. So, he asked for his due, and he received it.

The end of this tale leads to a broken young man who has "come to himself". Some versions translate this verse 17 as when he "came to his senses". While this is helpful, I believe it to be even more insightful to see in this verse the truth that the young man has come to see himself as he really was: unwise, prideful, angry, rebellious, etc.

How did the young man get to this point of seeing himself as he really was? Well, the Lord took him upon a journey in which he made poor choices and wasted his resources in wild spending on fast cars, hot women, and cold beer. Once the money was gone, so were his "friends". As he began to experience want and hunger, he had no option but to take a job which for him, a Jew, was repulsive and humiliating – the care and shepherding of swine. Only when his desperateness got to the point in which he was strategizing how to consume the pig slop for himself instead of giving it to the hogs was he able to see the lowlife of his personhood. Only then did he see his need for his father and for his father's family.

The truth is this: sometimes, the Lord has to take us into the pigsty via suffering in order to move us to the point in which we see our deep need for our Father and His Family.

Consider the Apostle Paul

As I have taught through the Book of Acts through the years, I have made an interesting discovery concerning the conversion of Saul/Paul in Acts 9.

Most of us have seen in Acts 8 (and have read in additional comments by Paul in his subsequent epistles) that Paul was an ambitious, arrogant, prideful, self-sufficient, self-righteous enemy of the Lord Jesus Christ and His Family.

Then came the road to Damascus.

I remember being taught in Sunday School that Paul was converted on this road to Damascus when he encountered the living resurrected Christ. You may have been taught the same thing. While I believe that my Sunday School teachers were unknowing and innocent in this, my study of the Scriptures has led me to the conclusion that my early teachers were in error.

It seems to me that if you read the ninth chapter of Acts carefully without this Sunday School presupposition, you will discover that the text actually teaches that Paul's conversion is described in verse 17-18. It was in the house on Straight Street (verse 11) that Paul was invaded by the Holy Spirit. It was here, in this house, where he heard from Ananias of the Sovereignty of the Lord Jesus in all of what had happened to him. It was here, in this house, when Paul experienced the power of the King. It was here, he was baptized.

What happened between the first encounter with Jesus on the road to Damascus and the ultimate conversion of Paul in the house at Straight Street? The answer: *blindness*.

This was the man who had been on the fast-track for Pharisee glory. He was a shoe-in for the Sanhedrin. He was destined to religious fame. Full of knowledge. Full of wisdom. Full of passion for Judaism. He was unstoppable. Also self-focused. Also self-reliant. Also self-centered.

Now, this same man has been struck helplessly blind – groping aimlessly, stumbling in humiliation, wandering around being led by others. We can only imagine his state-of-mind. Who is this Jesus who can do this to me? Who is this Jesus who can reduce me to nothingness? Who is this Jesus who can end all of my dreams in an instant? Who is this Jesus who choreographs others to come and minister to me? Who is this Jesus who can forgive me for what I have been doing to His followers? I now see my smallness. Who is this Jesus who has conquered death itself and now has conquered me?

It was the trauma of the suffering of the blindness (even if for only a few days) which the Lord used to bring Paul into the family of God. My suspicion is that none of the more subtle persuasive influences of the Gospel would have been sufficient for Paul. He was way too persuasive. He was way too cagy. Only the scalpel of suffering would be efficient to bring Paul to an end to himself so that he could see the glory of the Gospel.

Consider the Conversion of My Friend Jack

As my old friend Jack has shared with me his conversion to Jesus Christ, he has convinced me that the godly man that I have known for almost 30 years (one of the most "sold-out-to-Jesus" men that you will ever meet) was at one point in time a pretty hard-core-sinner. Jack will tell you, as he has told me, that God had to take him to the bottom of the barrel before Jack would see his need for Christ.

Jack shared with me a perspective years ago which I have never forgotten and which I have shared with others over the past three decades. Jack's teaching to me was that we can listen to the call of the Lord and come to Him easy or we can resist and He will keep coming after us until it gets really, well, "messy." In his Southern way, all theological sophistry aside, he would say that "God comes after us in a lot of different ways. But one way or another, He gets to us:

- First, He comes with a feather and tickles us to get our attention. If we don't listen then,
- Second, He comes with a ruler and slaps our hand, and it gets painful. If we don't listen then,
- Third, He comes with a 2x2, and it gets miserable. If we don't listen then,
- Finally, He comes with a 4x4 – and it gets messy."

Jack's perspective often reminded me of something which C.S. Lewis once wrote: "*God whispers to us in our pleasures, speaks in our conscience, but shouts in our pains; it is His megaphone to arouse a deaf world.*"[13]

Although I do not know all of the details, Jack has told me that he resisted, and God had to get him the hard way. Suffering was necessary for Jack to hear the call.

Consider the Conversion of My Friend Don

Prior to Don's conversion, if you had asked him the secret to success in his life, he would have told you that it had been hard work and good fortune. Don had always been a man of integrity, a man of commitment, a man of moral living, a man of his word, a man of patriotism – a hard-working individual who built his small business with nothing more than sweat and faithfulness.

Don's life was rolling along just like he wanted it to be. He had a beautiful home, a beautiful wife, three beautiful children, a healthy bank balance, and a growing and prosperous business. He was respected by almost everyone who knew him. He believed in God (in a generic sense) and was active in his church.

And then "calamity" struck. His wife up and announced that she was finished with him. She left him and their three children. To say that Don was devastated is a serious understatement of things. The foundation under his life collapsed.

I met Don about halfway through my 11-year tenure at my first church. I received a call from a fellow minister who recommended that I might want to disciple Don, who had just come to be a new Christian.

As Don has shared in his testimony, he had always been a man who could, just by the power of his will, make things happen as he liked. However, when his wife left him, he could not fix it. No matter what he did, he could not fix it. His children were slaughtered, and he could not fix it. There was a huge hole in the rhythm of his home, and he could not fix it. His wound was open for all to see, and he could not fix it.

It was this helplessness and hopelessness which led Don into brokenness. Brokenness led to openness. Although

Don had always believed in the existence of God and the value of His moral principles, Don had never entered into a personal relationship with Jesus. Don had never needed a Savior before. A friend shared the gospel with him, and Don fell into the arms of the Father.

Don will tell you even now that he probably would never have considered a personal relationship with Christ had it not been for the collapse of his marriage. His saying is this: "*Calamity is good in life; it took calamity to bring me to the Lord.*" It was the suffering that led Don to the cross and to his King.

As a side note, I have had the unbelievable privilege to disciple two adults (soon after their conversions) who were the most "on-fire" new believers I have ever worked with. Don was one of those two. He was hungry for Jesus in the most desperate ways. He was hungry for His Word. He was hungry to walk with Him and not just do the "church-thing". He was generous to the Kingdom beyond measure. Don wanted to serve and to love within the Kingdom of God.

As a P.S., God poured out upon Don Grace in more than one sense of the word. There was the Grace of his forgiveness and freedom in Christ. Then there was the other Grace, the wonderful godly woman whom the Lord blessed him with to be his lifetime partner in Christ.

Conclusion of the First D (Purpose) for Suffering: Deliverance

Why does the Lord choreograph and ordain specific suffering to be a part of the lives of specific people? Sometimes, He knows that the only way that some of us will ever consider Jesus is if He brings us to the end of ourselves. Paul will tell you. Jack will tell you. Don will tell you. Their experience of suffering was probably the only thing which would have led them to brokenness and then to openness to Him.

Some of us are so stubborn, so hard-headed, so strong-willed, and so rebellious, that only the sharp scalpel of suffering will bring us to our knees so that we become open to receive Jesus as our Lord and Savior.

Ask Paul, Jack, and Don when you get to heaven. I believe that they will tell you that their experiences of suffering were some of the greatest things which the Lord ever did for them. You see, the Lord knew them in the deep places of their souls – and the Master knew that for them – had there been no suffering, there would have been no salvation.

CHAPTER FIVE

The Second Purpose for Suffering: Discipline

Spare the Rod, Spoil the Child!
A "Close but no Cigar" Misquote of Scripture

It is for discipline that you endure; God deals with you as with sons; for what son is there whom his father does not discipline? But if you are without discipline, of which all have become partakers, then you are illegitimate children and not sons. Furthermore, we had earthly fathers to discipline us, and we respected them; shall we not much rather be subject to the Father of spirits, and live? For they disciplined us for a short time as seemed best to them, but He disciplines us for our good, that we may share His holiness. All discipline for the moment seems not to be joyful, but sorrowful; yet to those who have been trained by it, afterwards it yields the peaceful fruit of righteousness.
Hebrews 12: 7-11

In some respects, the second D is like the first D. In both of these first two purposes for sufferings, God's reason for choreographing and ordaining the suffering for a specific person is to bring him to see himself as a sinner in need of God's transforming grace. The difference in these two purposes for suffering orbits around the individual who is the divine target of the suffering.

The first D of suffering (Deliverance) is aimed at an unbeliever. God intends for the suffering to lead the unbeliever to brokenness and eventually to openness to hear of the free gift of Eternal Life which God the Father offers to him through the death and resurrection of His Son, Jesus Christ.

This second D of suffering (Discipline) is aimed at believers instead of unbelievers. This type of suffering pictures God as a Heavenly Father disciplining His children in His family.

Understanding the Nature of Discipline

Principle #1: Discipline is not Punishment

In order to get this discussion started on the right road, it is very important at the beginning to ascertain the biblical difference between discipline and punishment. I often have to discuss this difference in the parenting seminars because parents sometimes equate punishment and discipline. They are not the same.

Punishment is a military concept. It is the infliction of painful consequences upon our enemies, i.e. to punish them, defeat them, conquer them, disable them, make them pay.

Discipline, however, is a noun and verb of the family. Discipline is what we do to/for our children. Punishment is intended to crush and to demoralize. Discipline is intended to break, to redirect, and to rebuild.

In the arena of parenting of our children, both the Greek word for discipline (paidea) and the Hebrew word for discipline (musar) contain the balanced nuances of soft preventive discipline and of hard corrective discipline.

Preventive discipline includes the actions and influences which we take as parents which are designed to lead our children to healthy, godly, and desirable behaviors. Corrective discipline is what we do as parents to redirect our children's lives after our heirs have already demonstrated behavior which is undesirable.

It is the corrective discipline which is often confused with punishment. To be candid, sometimes the two may even outwardly appear similar, but the ultimate goal of each is worlds apart. Hebrews 12: 1-11 is crystal clear that the Lord's discipline is often painful and sorrowful at the point of impact. Like the rod or rebuke of a parent, the Lord's discipline may produce much anguish and suffering – even possibly to the point of the shedding of blood (12:4).

In Hebrews 12, the Lord helps us to understand that divine discipline and parental discipline have the same "ultimate goal" in that the final aim is the good of the person being disciplined. We need to nail this down deep in our hearts. Suffering may be used by the Lord to discipline His children, but it will never be a tool to "punish" His own.

Principle #2: God's Motive for Using Suffering as an Instrument of Discipline is Love

The motive for punishment is hate. The motive for discipline is love.

We can clearly see in Hebrews 12 that the motive of our God in using suffering as an instrument of discipline is love. It is His love of us as His children, not as illegitimate orphans (12: 6-8). He disciplines us because He claims us, He loves us, and He knows that our ways need to be altered or else we may become our own worst enemies.

In seminary, as an illustration, another student in our apartment complex had a feisty six-year-old daughter who had little regard for her father's instruction not to play in the street. During the middle of a study group, another child burst into the room with the news that this young princess was out in the middle of a busy highway in a large metropolitan city with a whistle from a crackerjack box and a police badge from the dollar store. She was holding up her hand and forcing traffic to stop. What do you think that father did?

He did not pass go. He did not collect $200. He sprinted at a breakneck speed to go to his daughter. You can pretty much bet there was some significant corrective discipline for that little girl, producing pain, grief, and tears.

Why did this father inflict this suffering upon his little girl? It is because his heart so loved his daughter that he knew he had to get her attention – and only the suffering of parental discipline seemed to get the job done. He cared for his princess. He wanted to protect his sweetheart from her own foolish ways and her own impish choices.

Principle #3: God's Goal for Disciplining His Children is Sanctification

What is this ultimate goal of Divine Discipline? What is Father's purpose? Again, Hebrews 12 helps us to understand that the Lord's purpose in suffering of this type is to bring about two fruits of sanctification into the life of the believer: holiness (vs. 10) and righteousness (vs. 11).

We need to get this right at the beginning. Our Father knows what we need, and He knows that sometimes we are our own worst enemies. Thus, He brings suffering into our lives, not to punish us for not getting it right, but to lead us to repentance and change, for our own sake and for our own future.

Understanding the Nature of Sanctification

People who have been raised with the meaty doctrines of Reformed Theology know the difference between justification, sanctification, and glorification.

So exactly what is sanctification? Sanctification is a lifelong process whereby the Holy Spirit works on believers to infuse or to implant righteousness into our lives. This is a gradual day-by-day transformation of the believer into the person whom the Lord has called us to be – whereby we slowly see our sin, we are broken about our sin, we repent of our sin, we become desperate again for the cleansing and transforming power of Christ's blood, and we plead again for His grace to change us. Little by little, He changes us.

I am ashamed to admit that for the longest time in my walk with the Lord, I did not understand how this sanctification process actually worked. Over the years, there have been three fundamental correctives which the Lord has led me to in my understanding of the nature of sanctification.

Corrective #1: Understanding Repentance, Brokenness and Helplessness

My first misunderstanding concerning sanctification orbited around my false view of my own works and my own human nature. My faulty logic went like this: Now that I am saved, I will get to know God's Word and what He desires of me, then I will do what He desires, then I will be living a more godly life, and then, finally, I will be more righteous. Or, to put it another way: learn the law, obey the law, develop a habit of obedience, mature spiritually, please God more, and become more righteous.

Unfortunately, I was viewing sanctification and spiritual growth exactly as the Apostle Paul warned us not to do in Galatians 3: 1-3. While I understood correctly that I was justified by faith and the Spirit, I was seeking to be sanctified by my works of the law. Just so you will know, this erroneous pathway to sanctification is ultimately both demoralizing and heretical.

The truth is that I can learn the law, but, at best, I can only obey at the most rudimentary external level. Two dangers exist. First, I might by the force of my will be able to obey this basic external manifestation of the law. If I can, then I am sorely tempted to the pride of the Pharisees. Second, I may well fail even at this basic level. If so, I then plummet down into despondency.

The fact is that I normally cannot even come close to obedience to the more exacting requirements of the law. True, I may succeed at not having a physical affair with another woman, but what man can pass the more demanding litmus test of lust of the eyes?

Please do not misunderstand me. Obeying the law is good and right, but the bottom line is that successfully obeying the basic external requirements of the law does not bring about the transformation of sanctification.

Transformation only begins to occur when I truly study the requirements of the law at such a deep level that I realize that I am way too flawed at my core to be completely faithful in my walk with Him. Eventually, the law makes us all see that we can never be totally obedient in the strength of our wills. Our disobedience saddens us because we see the depth of our sinfulness.

Ultimately, the seductive fundamental flaw of believing that we can be sanctified by our efforts, our obedience, our faithfulness, and our works is that we do not really need God to be transformed. We deceive ourselves to believe that we are capable of producing our spiritual growth all on our own. We become the "Elder Brother," as Tim Keller masterfully explains in his book, *The Prodigal God*.

This is where the rubber hits the road. Sanctification becomes a possibility only when we have been led by the Spirit to see our own spiritual bankruptcy. Bankruptcy leads to helplessness which leads to brokenness which leads to repentance which leads to pleas for transformation from the foot of the cross. Finally, we realize and confess that we need our God to make us different. Then, and only then, the Holy Spirit invades and transforms that portion of who we are which needs to be changed. You see, it is our brokenness and our desperateness which is the primordial ooze into which the Holy Spirit finds His fertile context for sanctification. And what does the Lord often use to take us into that brokenness – you guessed it: *suffering*.

Corrective #2: Understanding the Law of Undulation

In his classic book *The Screwtape Letters*, C. S. Lewis develops the idea of what he calls the "Law of Undulation."[14] The point of Lewis' assertion is that the forces of darkness want all of us believers to view the sanctification process of spiritual growth to look something like this:

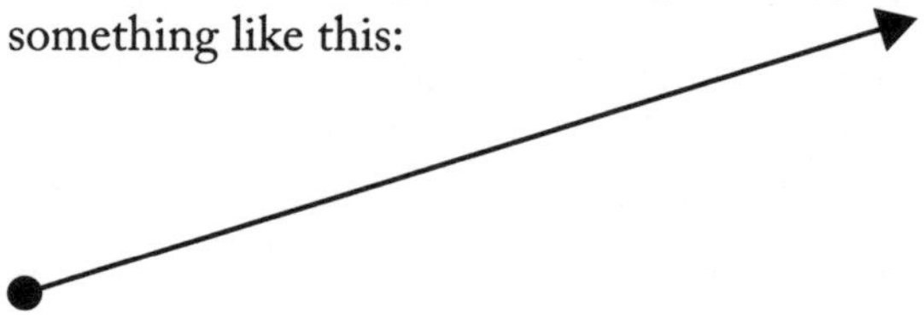

This flawed view of sanctification depicts a spiritual life which flows upward with only ups and no downs. We just keep doing good, and we just keep getting better and better. There is very little struggle with sin and very few dark times of any sort. As stated earlier, the desire of the darkness here is that this view of spiritual life will lead to either pride or despair. Either of which the darkness can use to pull us away from our loving Father.

But Lewis contends that the real picture of spiritual growth looks more like a squiggly line, and this he calls the Law of Undulation.

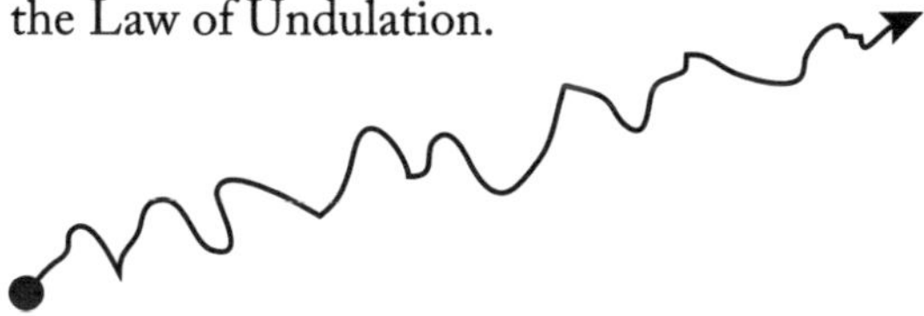

You will note the peaks of spiritual highs and the troughs of spiritual lows. There are times when life is good and God feels good. Let the good times roll! However, there are other times – the Wilderness Times – the times of suffering when things are hard, life is tough, and it is hard to discern His presence.

The question to be asked is this: When do we really grow in our intimacy with Him? When does sanctification growth occur? Is it in the peaks or the pits of our spiritual growth? Is it when life is great, our refrigerators are full, our marriages are fine, and our businesses are lucrative? Or is it when finances are tight, we need to pray for our daily bread, we need Him to provide for us a job, our spouse is a jerk, the diagnosis from the doctor is horrendous, and life looks bleak?

Well, look at the diagram. Where does the growth occur? We do not grow on the mountaintops. We grow in the pits/troughs. It is the hard times, the suffering times, the Wilderness Seasons, the Valley of the Shadow. These are the precursors to change, transformation, and growth.

Many of us wonder why that is. I did not get it until the Lord lead me to a third corrective.

Corrective #3: Understanding the Real Role of the Troughs in Life

Think of it like this. I often will ask the folks in my discipleship groups the following question. When do we see the farthest: during the daytime or during the nighttime?

The normal logical answer which I get to that question is this: we obviously see farther in the daytime when things are clear and not clouded with the shadows of dark. It certainly seems to be a reasonable answer. When I am hunting in the woods during the daytime, I sometimes can see clearly for 500 yards or more. At night, however, I may only be able to see a few yards in front of me.

The problem with this answer is that the scope of our perspective is too small. If we think big, it becomes clear pretty quickly that the actual correct answer is that we see much farther at night. Think about it. During the daytime, what is the farthest we can see? Answer: the sun. At night, however, we see much farther. We see the stars which are millions of light years beyond our sun.

If we can translate this into our discussion on sanctification, when can we really see the long-range (can I use the word "eternal") big picture of life's issues? Do we see the eternal things best on the hilltops when life is good and the light of daytime is everywhere? Or do we see the eternal things best in the Valley of the Shadow times of darkness and suffering?

I hope that the answer is obvious. We see the "big picture" of the spiritual paradigm so much more clearly in the Valley of the Shadow. It is there where we understand more succinctly the things of the Kingdom. It is there where we see more clearly the things which will truly pass the test of time. It is there where we taste of the real things of eternity. It is there where we intimately meet God. It is in the troughs and pits of life in which we see the "big landscape" of our life's purposes and we have the greatest openness to God's design for our lives.

I believe that God knows that when we need to be turned from our sin and moved further down the road of sanctification, we need to experience the scalpel of suffering. He loves us enough to take us into the Valley of the Shadow so that we can see the important changes which He knows need to be made in our lives. The Lord often uses the experience of suffering in our lives to discipline us because the Valley of the Shadow is the only place where we will see the "big picture" and listen to Him.

Some Illustrations from Scripture

There are a plethora of biblical pictures of the Lord using suffering to discipline His children and to thus call those believers to the road of growth and maturity.

Consider the case of the sister of Moses, Miriam

In Numbers 12: 1-15, we find Miriam (as well as Aaron) in some pretty deep sin. She is jealous of her brother Moses and the place of spiritual influence to which the Lord had placed Moses. She "spoke against" Moses, and questioned his integrity and his right to be God's instrument for the Lord's purposes.

The Lord Yahweh was not happy about that at all. He admonishes Miriam, and then the Lord strikes her with advanced leprosy. In those days, leprosy was basically the "blackball" of life – the rotting flesh, the body parts falling off, the stench to burn your nostrils, the separation from all of the rest of God's People, the shame of running around everywhere screaming at the top of your lungs the crowd-dispersing words "Unclean, Unclean." Life as Miriam had known it was over.

In His Grace to His daughter, Miriam, the Master only allowed her to suffer for seven days. However, apparently one week of leprosy was the trick. It was enough to cure Miriam of her criticisms, her "bad reports", her back-stabbing, and her grumbling heart.

Consider the case of the prophet Jonah

Jonah was a hard-headed, rebellious, stubborn, prideful, judgmental, arrogant, and disobedient preacher. The Lord called Jonah and gave him a mission to go due east to Nineveh. After this clear call from His God, Jonah went as fast as his little prophet feet could take him in the opposite direction – due west to Tarshish.

Run, Jonah, run! Head on *down* to Joppa, *down* into the ship, *down* into the hold of the ship, and eventually *down* into the Mediterranean Sea. (Did you notice the direction which disobedience takes us?) The truth is that, like Jonah, believers who are in sin "can run but they just can't hide." God sent a storm to rein in Jonah from his sin. The experience of being thrown overboard and almost meeting his end in the ocean blue left Jonah pretty desperate for God to show up – which He did when He sent the big fish.

When I teach and preach on Jonah, I note that Jonah still had sin-struggles even after the storm. But the man who washed up on the shores of Nineveh looking all bleached-out and smelling like whale vomit was no longer a man running away from his call to preach to the Assyrians. Maybe it was a little too much "hellfire and brimstone" for some of our tastes, but the man preached it with passion.

Miriam listened to the Lord when the darkness of leprosy was brought upon her by her God. Jonah was desperate for His King when he was going down for the third time. Like many of us, the suffering of the Lord hitting us over the head with a 4x4 is the only way we will listen to the Lord.

The Caution

We do not want to make the mistake of Job's advisors!

It is true that sometimes the Lord's purpose of choreographing suffering into our life is that God is seeking our *Deliverance.* He is bringing the Valley of the Shadow upon us so that we will be broken over our sin and turn to Christ for forgiveness and eternal life. Please let me say this as clear as I can: It is always appropriate for someone enduring suffering to ask themselves the "big money" questions about their eternal relationship with the Lord.

It is also true that sometimes the Father permits suffering into our life for the purpose of the *Discipline* of believers and calling us to repentance for our particular sin or sins. The Lord is utilizing suffering to help us see the "big picture" and to lead us into brokenness and further dependence upon Christ for the life of faith. Again, I want us to hear that it is always appropriate and right for those of us who are believers and who are undergoing suffering to examine ourselves deeply for areas of sin in our lives to which God has focused His magnifying glass.

However, the error of Job's advisors was the presumption that these were the only two possible explanations for suffering. Clearly Job was a believer. Thus, the only conceivable explanation for Job's emotional and physical suffering at the hands of Satan must surely be that the believer Job had sin for which God was disciplining him.

Please know, my friends, that while it is always appropriate to allow the valley times of the Law of Undulation to be times for us to examine ourselves for sin, there are at least three additional explanations for suffering which have little to nothing to do with our sin as individual believers.

The next three chapters highlight these three Ds (purposes) for suffering which are not necessarily brought upon us because of our particular sin or sins.

CHAPTER SIX

The Third Purpose for Suffering: Development

To ask that God's love should be content with us as we are is to ask that God should cease to be God; because He is what He is, His love must, in the nature of things, be impeded and repelled by certain stains in our present character, and because He already loves us He must labour to make us loveable.
C.S. Lewis[15]

In this you greatly rejoice, even though now for a little while, if necessary, you have been distressed by various trials, that the proof of your faith, being more precious than gold which is perishable, even though tested by fire, may be found to result in praise and glory and honor at the revelation of Jesus Christ.
1 Peter 1: 6-7

Sometimes our Father choreographs suffering into our lives at times when there is no apparent correlation between the suffering and any particular sin in our life of which we need to repent. This purpose for suffering *(Development)* is the first of three divine explanations for suffering in our lives which often appear to be unrelated to our particular sins. Sometimes the Lover of our souls goes with us through the Valley of the Shadow in order to develop and to prepare us for what lies ahead.

An Illustration from Nature

Whenever I teach upon this particular reason for God choreographing suffering into the fabric of our lives, I usually begin with this word picture from nature. I believe that it was probably sometime in my Junior High years in science class when I first was taught where pearls come from.

If I was taught correctly, the process begins when a grain of sand enters into the sensitive tender mucous lining of the oyster. Like many of our suffering experiences, this dynamic enters the oyster's existence and begins to slice, dice, fluster, irritate, aggravate, and generally make the oyster's life painful and miserable.

In ways which I do not completely understand, the oyster responds to this instrument of suffering in such a manner that the Lord causes a gradual development to occur which ultimately results in a pearl to be created in the very inner tender lining of the oyster.

For my money, this word picture is helpful as I think about the Father's plan to develop us through the process of suffering. There are instruments of suffering which He orchestrates to infiltrate into our lives. Some of these instruments are small and some are huge, but they all are painful.

It seems to me that we can learn a lot from the oyster. The Lord has an ultimate design in these cases of development to take that instrument of suffering and to use it to produce "pearls of character" in the very tender linings of our souls. Apparently, we can attempt to resist the process and commit ourselves to eliminate the instrument of suffering from our existence at all costs, or we can accept the instrument of suffering from the hand of God and rejoice in His ministry of pearl-making in our character.

These pearls are the fruit of His "development" of our personhood.

The Teachings of Scripture on Development

All three of these passages below teach a pattern of development which hopefully will flow from the tribulation-trial-testing events of our lives. Often, our seasons of suffering constitute a trial and/or a temptation of our spiritual constitution. The goal line of all of these development Scriptures depict the final products or the pearls of this divine pattern: proven character, proven faith, maturity, hope, glory to God.

	Romans 5:3-5	James 1:2-4	Peter 1: 6-7
Attitude:	exult in tribulations	have joy in trials	rejoice in trials
Process:	perseverance	endurance	tested by fire
Pearl:	proven character	maturity in personhood	proves faith imperishable
Blessing:	hope	--	glory to Christ

Let us explore two aspects of the teachings of these texts.

The First Aspect to Explore: Two Competing Agendas

What is the meaning of this word which is translated here as "tribulation or trial"? It is actually somewhat interesting to study the actual Greek words inspired by the Holy Spirit in these passages.

The word utilized in the Romans 5 passage is *thelipsesin* (in the Greek) which is best translated as an affliction or tribulation resulting in mental and/or spiritual distress brought about by "outward circumstances."[16]

While the thrust of the Romans 5 passage indicates that the hopeful goal for the believer is that this tribulation will ripen into perseverance and then proven character, there is a secondary meaning of *thelipsesin* which links these tribulations to a darker path. Rather than leading to hope, it is possible that *thelipsesin* may indeed lead one into a state akin to imprisonment and bondage.

This implication that tribulations may either lead to hope in our Lord or to bondage on the other hand is confirmed by the meaning of the Greek word used in the other two passages.

Both James 1 and 1 Peter 1 utilize the word *peirazo*[17] which has two distinct meanings: (1) to put one to the test; or (2) to tempt or entice one to sin. Here is what is so interesting about this word.

Normally, when the word is describing the action of God, it is translated as "test" which implies that it is the desire of the Lord for believers to endure and to mature through this difficult time.

However, normally when the word is describing the action of Satan or his ambassadors, then the word is usually translated as "tempt." This is an endeavor designed to seduce us into sin.

I believe that the bottom line when it comes to these tribulations choreographed by our Father (for our development) is that there are two competing agendas percolating at the same time:

First, there is the agenda of the Lord for us to endure the suffering and thus mature and become stronger in our trust in Him. The purpose of this kind of suffering is that we will trust Father, draw close to Father, and be refined by Father as He uses the fire to purify us and to produce the pearls.

Second, there is the agenda of the darkness for us to be seduced to the "dark side," to stand on our own rather than draw close to the Lord, and to fail the test – thus, resulting in a wilting in the believer's ministry in the Kingdom of God. To be succinct, Satan desires to put believers on the sidelines of the War of Wars by convincing them that the Lord cannot be trusted and that they are hopeless and powerless failures.

The Second Aspect to Explore: Another Dynamic of Sanctification

What does this pattern of development look like when our Father's agenda prevails without us first sinning and falling prey to the agenda of darkness? (Of course, if we do sin, we may be back to the divine agenda of "*Discipline.*")

It is helpful to make a connection here between this pattern of development described in the three passages above and our earlier discussion of sanctification in the earlier chapter on Discipline. The goal of sanctification as discussed in the earlier chapter is that we become the healthy, godly, and mature believers whom God has designed us to be (following Christ into the War of Wars against darkness). Looking at the three passages at the beginning of this chapter, where do these seasons of tribulations ultimately lead us if we draw close to the Lord and allow Him to develop us?

Here is the goal line or the "character pearls" according to these three passages:

- Romans 5: proven character
- James 1: maturity in personhood
- 1 Peter 1: proven faith

The goal line of this development process sounds a great deal like the goal of the sanctification process! That really should not surprise us.

If we can recall the discussion of the *Law of Undulation* in the previous chapter on Discipline, we can be reminded that we see the "big picture" (the eternal perspective) of life better in the dark times of suffering. This "big picture" grabs the souls of believers at a deeper level. We endure the experience of the suffering at the moment of its affliction, and we wait for the Lord to develop us in greater strength, greater faith, and greater maturity.

This time the growth which emerges from the Valley of the Shadow does not come from the Holy Spirit leading us to repentance concerning our sin. Rather, the growth and maturation comes as the Lord walks with us through the season of suffering and we find that we trust (faith) Him even more than before, and then we discover that we have been transformed (little bit by little bit). We have been made stronger in the faith, more mature in our walk with Him, and more fruitful for His Kingdom. He has changed us!

At the risk of over-simplifying this development process, I would like to offer you a second analogy or word picture. When I was in high school, I was into athletics pretty deeply (wrestling, football, etc.). One of the things which all of my coaches in all of my sports focused upon was "weight training".

To be candid, pumping iron was not one of my favorite things to do, but I understood that it was a necessary component of my development. Thus, I needed to both embrace and endure such training. However, the one thing that I did like about the weight training regiment was the teenage boy vanity event of looking in the mirror immediately after a workout. Our arms were swollen, and we looked like Olympian body-builders in our own minds. We would all look in the mirror in the training room and angle this way, then turn that way, then do a flex poise. Man, we looked tough!

What I did not know then was that the training regimen of lifting weights actually tears at the fibers of the muscles in our arms and legs. The muscle fibers are ripped apart.

If the fibers in our muscles could talk, they would scream out in desperation – Stop! Stop! This is awful! We are in a valley of the shadow down here. Bad and gruesome things are happening to us. This is suffering for no apparent purpose. This is horrible… *please make it stop!*

Actually, that pumped up look immediately following a hard workout is really our bodies sending healing fluids to our muscle fibers in response to their screams for help.

Now, why did my coaches make me subject my poor, little, innocent muscle fibers to such suffering, pain and anguish? If I correctly understand the physiology of our bodies, the answer as to why our coaches thought this was a good idea is because of what our body does in response to this muscle fiber suffering.

Following the fiber suffering event, all of that fluid and stuff which our body sends to our fibers gets in between the wounded fibers and begins the healing process. The end result (via a transformation process which is way above my pay grade) is that somehow new muscle fiber is created. This results in a muscle which has been changed and now has more substance causing the entire arm or leg to actually become stronger than it was before the fiber suffering event.

I could bench press 140 pounds when I started as a sophomore. As a senior, I could bench press 220 pounds – more fiber, more muscle, stronger.

The Lord's purpose of developing believers via suffering has a lot of commonalities with weight lifting. His sanctification objective is to make us *stronger* in His Way: our character is proven, we are made more mature, and our faith is proven imperishable.

Why do we need this kind of Development?

A common response on this teaching about "suffering for development" is this: "Well, Dr. Childs, I believe that I am perfectly happy without all of this development stuff. Why is it so necessary for the Lord to be doing all of this developing of His believers? Doesn't He love me the same regardless of whether I can lift 140 pounds or 220 pounds? Why can't He just leave us alone? Why must we go through the pain? If it is all the same to Him, I think that I will just pass. Please tell Him to make it stop!"

It is right here at this specific point where we can see the crux of the difference between the biblical perspective on suffering and the heretical "health and wealth" churches which I referred to earlier.

The perspective of the "health and wealth" teachers is that everything in our relationship with God orbits around the understanding that everything is about us. The purpose of us having a saving relationship with God is so that God can give us everything we need (as we define what we need for ourselves). It is all about God wanting us to have a really great life here on earth. Therefore, He will protect us from any and all suffering. Because it is all about us, He will give us the Yellow Brick Road to walk so that absolutely nothing undesirable will happen to us. Do right by Him and He will treat you right. With this paradigm, of course, we tell our God to cease and desist any painful development. We know what we need to have a pleasurable life, and development via suffering ain't on our list.

Peter Kreeft takes serious issue with these 'health-and-wealthers' and their teachings: "*The point of our lives in this world is not comfort, security, or even happiness, but training; not fulfillment, but preparation.*"[18]

I do not think that I can find a better place to stand to express my disagreement with the 'health-and-wealthers' concerning the purpose for which we have been called into His Kingdom than to remind us of the answer to the first catechism question:

Q1. What is the chief end of man?
To glorify God and enjoy Him forever.

It should be self-evident that this relationship which we have with Him is not all about us. Rather, it is all about Him. We glorify Him. He does not serve us. We draw close to enjoy Him. We worship Him. We serve Him. We join His family. We enlist to fight in His army. We follow Him into the battles of His war against the spiritual forces of darkness.

Friends, this is a fundamental biblical principle with which we must come to grips. If it is all about us, then we should be the one determining if we should taste of suffering. If it is all about Him, however, then if He desires to develop us further through suffering, then we submit to His decision and climb up in His arms to go through the Valley of the Shadow.

Why might God want to develop us further? There may be a number of reasons, as I will try to enumerate below.

The First Possible Reason for Development: "Battlefield Triage"

2 Cor 1: 3-4 tells us that He develops us through suffering because He wants to use us in the future to minister to others:

> *Blessed be the God and Father of our Lord Jesus Christ, the Father of mercies and God of all comfort; Who comforts us in all our affliction so that we may be able to comfort those who are in any affliction with the comfort with which we ourselves are comforted by God.*

In my thirty years of pastoral experience, I have found as a rule that when someone in our flock begins to experience some form of suffering, they will usually draw closer to others who have gone through similar deep dark times.

I remember early in ministry when a woman in our church family was diagnosed with breast cancer and was facing a mastectomy. This strong Christian woman went into a tailspin. Deep depression set in. She would not let anyone (including her husband and her pastor, who was me) to help her. It was through this pretty painful season that both her husband and I learned an important lesson: women with breast cancer who experience surgical removals almost always can only be comforted by other woman who have experienced the same. She was surrounded by people who loved her, but she felt no one could possibly understand the pain, the confusion, the shame, the loss of self-esteem unless they themselves had gone through it.

I do not know why so many of us are like that, but it does seem to be part of our human nature. After losing Clete and going through the dark trauma of grief recovery (although you never actually recover), I have found more and more people bringing their grief issues and other deep suffering issues to my doorstep. They usually ask me two or three similar questions:

- *How do you get through it?* That is when I usually talk about crawling up in His arms and just letting Him carry me through the Valley of the Shadow.
- *Will it ever get better?* I usually tell them that some things get better, but there are other things which are changed for the rest of this life on earth (notice that I did not say that they are changed forever.)
- *Why did God let this happen to me?* I usually tell them about how He has taught me about these five Ds (purposes) for suffering.

The important point, however, is not that I might have a few naive piddling answers. The important point is that people who are suffering almost always go to others who have experienced suffering.

So why does our Father develop us by further suffering? One reason is because He is training us to do "battlefield triage" ministry to help our brothers and sisters in Christ who are wounded by their sufferings. Often, we may be the first line of defense in a long list of people whom the Lord may use to heal and to restore our wounded comrades.

The Second Possible Reason for Development: Warriors for His War

He may wish to develop us through suffering because He desires stronger and healthier warriors in His War against darkness. He wants fierce warriors who trust Him and will draw close to Him when the arrows of spiritual darkness are targeted for us. He desires maturity in His army.

While I know that this is changing the analogy, I believe that John 15 helps me a lot with understanding this kind of development. Jesus tells us in the beginning of this chapter of John that He is the vine, we are the branches, and Father is the vinedresser.

In this analogy, apparently the vinedresser (God the Father) finds the healthy branches that are bearing fruit and prunes them (15:2). While I am not in the wine-making business and I have never been a vinedresser, I have done a little study of this passage, and I have discovered that the commentaries are pretty consistent in their understanding of why the vinedresser does what He does. Here are some key observations:

- If the fruitful branch could talk, he would scream out: Stop! Stop! This is killing me. This is suffering. My limb is cut off and my branch bleeds. This is Valley of the Shadow. This can't be good. Please stop now.

- The vinedresser actually knows what He is doing. Even though some of the growths on the healthy branch are viable, good in themselves, and will grow to fruition, the vinedresser prunes them off so that in the long run, the branch will grow bigger, better, and more fruit.
- The best wines come from vines which have a vinedresser Who knows what He is doing.

Let me see if I can help make a connection with this analogy of the pruning of the vinedresser and the development of Kingdom warriors for the spiritual battlefield of the War of Wars. Grapes and Army enlistees may share a great deal in common.

I like to talk a lot with friends in our fellowship about following Jesus (our Warrior King) to fight in the War of Wars. We believe that this War was started and defined in Genesis 3:15 – the curse of the enmity (hatred, war) placed upon the serpent. We believe that our Warrior King is the One promised in this text. He is the Champion who will be struck in the heel by the serpent (the Crucifixion) and who will crush the serpent's head (the Resurrection).

This War is further depicted in 2 Kings 6:17 when the Lord revealed His legions of horses and chariots of fire to the fearful servant. This is the other side of the tapestry of the War of Wars.

Ephesians 6: 10-21 describes this War as follows:

> *For our struggle is not against flesh and blood, but against the rulers, against the powers, against the*

> *world forces of this darkness, against the spiritual forces of wickedness in the heavenly places.*

Now, I am an old U.S. Army Infantry Platoon Leader from years gone by. I know a fair amount about the military and about training for war. I know that the very first thing that has to be done is to get the soldier into physical shape. That is one of the primary reasons why Boot Camp exists. Getting into Boot Camp shape requires a great deal of suffering for the young trainees. Even after Boot Camp, the Army felt that it was important to keep its soldiers in top physical shape. I can still remember those 4:45am twelve mile runs – suffering indeed!

Why does the military submit their soldiers to such suffering? In the long run, it is because the military knows that the soldier needs that training in order to be developed for war: in order to be made stronger, to be made healthier, to be made better. That strength and might will be what enables them to survive and to follow the Lord into His conquests on the battlefield.

As pruning produces the finest wine from a particular vine, so suffering is often the spiritual process by which the Lord makes pearls out of grains of sands, diamonds out of lumps of coal, and soldiers out of enlistees.

There is an old story from the lips of a blacksmith which has helped me understand this purpose of development:

> *A blacksmith known for his strong faith had a great deal of illness. He was challenged by an unbeliever to explain why his God would let him suffer.*

> *He explained, "I take a piece of iron, put it into the fire to bring it to a white heat, then I strike it once or twice to see if it will take temper. I plunge it into water to change the temperature, put it into the fire again, then I put in on the anvil and make a useful article out of it. If it will not take temper when I first strike it on the anvil I throw it into the scrap heap and sell it for a half-penny per pound.*
>
> *"I believe God has been testing me to see if I will take temper. I have tried to bear it as patiently as I could, and my daily prayer has been, 'Lord, put me into the fire if you will; put me into the water if you think I need it; do anything, you please, O Lord, only don't throw me on the scrap heap'."*

The second possible reason why the Lord may be developing us is that He is forging a "warrior of steel" whom He will lead into the battle against darkness. This is a warrior who has been pruned resulting in the finest of her possibilities. She has been tempered and molded into the strongest that she can be for His War of Wars. In the fires of her suffering, she has learned that she can trust her Warrior King with everything and that she can follow Him anywhere. He has developed her. He has refined her. The 90 pound weakling is no more, and she has become a lean, mean, fighting machine (you know, in the right kind of spiritual sense). May we with Calvin remember that we "must submit to supreme suffering in order to discover the completion of joy."[19]

The Third Possible Reason for Development: The Need for Generals

It is interesting to me to note in the scriptures that, more often than not, when the Lord has set His eye upon someone whom He intends to develop into a leader or General for His War of Wars, He usually takes them through a development process of hardship which gradually leads to leadership.

When Samuel (see 1 Samuel 16) was lead to Jesse as the father whose son would be the king to succeed Saul, none of the older sons passed the Lord's muster. However, the youngest of the sons (David) was out in the fields tending to Jesse's sheep. From that vocation, the Lord would call him to lead and to shepherd the People of God.

It also seems that when Moses was called to be the leader of the People of God, he also was tending to the flocks of his father-in-law, Jethro (Exodus 3:1).

The truth is that I have very little first-hand knowledge of the "opportunities" for development which may arise as one is tasked with the responsibilities to tend to flocks of sheep. What I have read, however, has led me to believe that shepherds of old break down into two basic groups: the lazy and the diligent. I have been led to believe that the great majority of shepherds of old fall into the lazy group. Because that appears to be the norm, the diligent shepherd is noteworthy.

The diligent shepherd who truly cares for his flock and defends his flock often finds the task to be grueling, including hours and hours of sleeplessness watching for the enemies of the flock. It also involves the constant wandering spirit of the individual sheep, the lengthy searching for the lost sheep, the unending conflict between the alpha ewes within the flock and their desire to be the "boss" of the flock.

I cannot help but think that the long sleepless nights with the self-centered "feed me" sheep of Jethro's flock must have been the Lord's development of Moses and preparation of him to lead through the wilderness the whining, complaining, "feed me", me-centered, rebellious, and fickle flock known as the People of God.

Because this whole "human leadership" in the Kingdom of God is a personal soap box of mine, I will try to be brief. In both covenant families and the militant church of Jesus, I have found a noted lack of leadership. I probably need to write a separate book on this matter. We do not see many real leaders anymore. What we see instead are *politicians* – husbands trying to appease family members and church leaders (pastors, as well as elders) who are seeking just to keep everybody happy.

Too often, we no longer see many men who know where the Lord is leading their families and then emerge out of their 'stay safe' foxholes and lead their families with a winsome battle cry of "follow me!"

Too often, we no longer see elders and pastors who do much more than pacify those members who tend to be the "squeaky wheels" demanding "feed me!" Consequently, many churches become "consumer-oriented" rather than "ministry-oriented". Everyone is happy, but not much real Kingdom work is being done.

There are so few real leaders – which in my personal opinion probably explains why the church today is so generally ineffective at having any influence whatsoever upon the darkness of the culture around them.

I am sorry. I digress. But maybe one of the reasons we have such a vacuum of leadership in our homes and in our churches today is precisely because we have lost all perspective on a healthy theology of suffering.

The bottom line is that we need leaders today to follow the King of Kings and then lead our families and our churches into the War of Wars against darkness. *I believe that the ones who are called by the Warrior King to such leadership responsibilities have been developed and refined and reformed by Him through a plethora of trials and tribulations. It is true: no pain, no gain.*

These are the Generals who have become the men and women of many pearls.

Summary: The Purpose of Development

This has been a long chapter trying to help each of us understand why the Lord might choreograph suffering into our lives when there does not appear to be a particular sin for which we can identify, confess, repent, take to the cross, and find grace and mercy.

We have looked at some of the biblical texts. We have reflected again upon the sanctification process. We have tried to think of possible ministries for which the Master might be preparing us (which would require deeper development and richer maturity). We have tried to understand this purpose of suffering from a number of different perspectives:

- the analogy of weight-lifting leading to stronger muscle tissue.
- the illustration of the pruning of the vine-dresser which results in finer wines.
- the word picture of the oyster and the grain of sand which produces "character pearls" within our souls; and
- the parallel of a blacksmith forging an instrument of steel in the fire.

Whatever analogy or metaphor we might choose to focus upon, the core dynamic always comes back to this: when suffering occurs for which we cannot see any connection to our personal sinfulness, we often may not see the immediate purpose for our development and the only real option available to us is to crawl up into the arms of our Savior and trust that He knows what He is doing as He leads His children through what comes to us as the battles of life.

CHAPTER SEVEN

The Fourth Purpose for Suffering: Deployment

I shall be telling this with a sigh
Somewhere ages and ages hence:
Two roads diverged in a wood, and I –
I took the one less traveled by,
And that has made all the difference.
Robert Frost, "The Road Not Taken"

And as for you, you meant evil against me, but God meant it for good in order, to bring about this present result, to preserve many people alive.
Genesis 50: 20

The Fourth D (or purpose) for suffering is *Deployment*. Deployment is a military term which means to be sent from where you are in a new direction to accomplish a new mission.

This suffering is the second kind of God's purposes in our suffering which may have little to nothing to do with particular sins in our life.

The principle is this: Sometimes the direction of our life, our vocation, where we live, the ministry we are in, the relationships we have – all these things are all good, right, and honorable. There is nothing wrong, sinful, or evil with where we are, what we are doing, why we are doing it, or who we are doing it with. But, for reasons known only to the Supreme Commander of the Universe, the Lord God wants to move us, to relocate us, or to place us upon a new trajectory, a new direction, a new mission, a new ministry.

The new call which He will give us will clearly be biblically permissible and will not in any way require us to sin, but we may have no clue as to why God is taking us there or why the King believes that this new trajectory is better than the old one. Possibly, we may see later why God moved us like He did, but there is no biblical mandate that God is required to reveal this to us.

The Biblical Example

It seems self-evident to me that Joseph in the Old Testament is a classical picture of God choreographing suffering into a believer's life in order to redirect his paths, put him into another place, and to use him in another mission which God felt was important. The account of Joseph and how the Warrior King worked in and through his life is found in Genesis chapters 37-50.

In his original setting, Joseph was one of the "fair-haired children" of his father – one of the favorites of his dad, Israel (Jacob) (37:3). He was the son of a wealthy land-owner who was living in the Promised Land, and who was right smack in the center of what the Lord God was doing here on the earth. Joseph's future looked so bright (as the old commercial says), he needed shades. His future was set: he would be a land baron with tremendous influence and significant wealth and possessions.

Now at the age of 17, Joseph apparently had to make a truthful, necessary, but ultimately unfavorable report on some of the activities of his older brothers (37:2) to his dad. Not long after that, apparently God gave Joseph a couple of dreams of what was to come, which included Joseph being raised up to a position of prominence superseding the prominence of others in his family.

While there are some commentaries which imply that Joseph may have been prideful in his interpretation of those dreams (which would be pretty normal for most 17 year old boys), I do not actually see that explicitly taught in the scriptures. I do not see anything in the Word of God which would indicate that God took the action which He did with Joseph in order to persuade Joseph to repent of any such sin of pride.

Instead (as we see in Genesis 50: 20), the scriptures teach that God took these actions in order to preserve the lives of the entire family – the entire clan of His People.

We need to back up, however, and try to see this from Joseph's perspective. In Joseph's original context, there was nothing sinful about where Joseph was, what he was doing, how he was doing it, or why he was doing what he was doing. It was the life God had given him, and it was good!

And then, boom! His brothers accosted him, imprisoned him in some pit, and then sold him into slavery to some Midianite traders. As in the old television sitcom, "You are my wife, good bye city life, Green Acres we are there!,"

Joseph was ripped from his home, his family, and everyone and everything he had ever known.

Now, try to imagine what Joseph's conversation with the Lord may have sounded like as Joseph rides in the back of the wagon wearing his new chains. *Lord, why has this suffering come upon me? What have I done to deserve this kind of treatment from Your hand? This is not good. This is Valley of the Shadow. My entire life is passing away before my eyes. Do something, my Lord, make this stop and make this right!*

But the Lord did not change anything in Joseph's suffering. Instead, the Warrior King allowed matters eventually to get even worse for Joseph.

Sold to an Egyptian officer named Potiphar, Joseph's gifts and abilities are highlighted by the Lord and Joseph rises to the position of the "house manager" (kind of a Chief of Staff) of Potiphar's affairs (45:1-6).

However, Joseph was a handsome physical specimen to behold. As the old song says, he was too sexy for his shirt (a contemporary translation of 39: 6). It wasn't his fault that he looked good with his shirt off. After all, he was just a good-looking, strong, healthy young man in his late teens or early twenties. However, Potiphar's wife (have you noticed that the Lord does not even allow her personal name to be recorded for posterity's sake?) gets the hots for him and makes a move on him.

Now what does Joseph do? Has he, in his anger toward God for all of this unjust suffering of his slavery, decided to cast off all of the principles of holiness of his God? Does he participate in this fornication? No, he makes the godly choice, the right choice, the holy choice, the biblical choice.

OK, now God is going to step in and clean up all of this messy suffering stuff. Now, God is going to make things right. Now, God is going to restore Joseph to his rightful place? Right? *Wrong!*

Joseph makes the right choice and what does it get him? His trajectory gets worse. His life is now not only one of a slave, but he is put into prison. Now this is not the prison of today with its central air, recreation yards, and running water for the toilets. No, this is the prison of old with rats, roaches, no beds, and no outdoor privileges.

I wish that I could hear Joseph's conversation with the Lord now. I know how it would probably go with me and maybe with you:

> *Alright, Lord, I have just about had it with You. I accepted the slavery stuff without a lot of complaining. I did not think it was fair, but I deferred to Your Divinity perspective, and I gave You the benefit of the doubt. But You have crossed the line with this latest development! I might could understand my being in prison if I had slept with that woman. I could understand that You were disciplining me. But, my King, I made the right choice, I did the right thing, I did what You have said is good. And what did it get me? This stupid, rat-infested, urine-saturated, toxic prison cell. I trusted You, and now my life is over. I have*

> *no future. I have no one to love me. I have no reason to live!*

That is probably how most of us would have reacted. However, even though the Lord does not record Joseph's responses to his landing in prison, the rest of Joseph's life makes me suspect that Joseph may have done a better job of reacting to God's choreography of his suffering than most of us might have responded.

The long and short of it is this: God maneuvered him to be in prison so that Joseph could interpret the chief cupbearer's dream. Then the dominos would start to fall for Joseph. He would interpret Pharaoh's dream; then he would rise to become the "Chief of Staff" of Pharaoh's kingdom. At the young age of thirty, Joseph was the second most powerful man in all of Egypt (41: 38-46).

Now, why did the Lord change Joseph's trajectory? Why did God send Joseph upon this decade-long journey of unbelievable suffering? Why did the Supreme Commander of the Universe utilize suffering in order to deploy Joseph to Egypt?

Because God knew what He was doing! Joseph's high position in Egypt would be the necessary position from which he would eventually house and protect all of the Family of God (Israel and all of his seed) from certain death from the vast long-term famine in the region.

Real Life Applications

I suspect that this kind of suffering is the hardest kind of suffering to understand when we are in the middle of it. While God is weaving His tapestry upon the canvas of our lives, all we see is the backside with all of its loose ends and dangling strings which make absolutely no sense to us.

All we can see is the way life was and could have been. We cannot see the big picture which may only emerge at the end of the tunnel. I have seen this in real life: in the life of others, but sometimes in the orbit of my own life, too.

The Boll Weevil

I have been told that the city of Enterprise, Alabama is the only city on the face of the earth where we can find a monument to an insect: the infamous boll weevil. I remember my father driving through this city and pointing out this Boll Weevil monument, and I remember asking my dad the question which I am sure many children have asked over the decades: *Dad, why did they erect a monument to a bug?*

My dad explained it like this. This area of southeast Alabama was famous for its cotton fields for centuries going back to the 1700s. It was the production of cotton which supported the entire economy of this area. It was the cotton plantations which were the backbone of the life of this part of the state.

One year, the boll weevil showed up in our corner of the cotton world. Son, he explained to me, the boll weevil eats and destroys the cotton plants. Farmers had untold losses of cotton acreage. Family plantations wobbled upon their financial legs. The economy of the Wiregrass area, as it is called, held its breath.

The next year, the boll weevil returned and the results were economically catastrophic.

Well, in the third year, the farmers and plantation owners knew that they had to do something different and they desperately planted other crops in the hope of making a living. In this process of experimenting with new crops, the farmers in this area discovered a miracle crop which grew fruitfully in this area. In fact, the farmers and plantation owners made much more profit with this new crop than they ever dreamed of making while raising cotton. The new crop was peanuts. That is why the Wiregrass area of southeast Alabama is known now as the peanut capital of the world to this day, claiming to produce more peanuts than anyplace else on the planet.

After a few years, the farmers in this area realized that the boll weevil had done the economy of this area a tremendous favor by bringing its ravaging plague upon their crops. They were better off and wealthier because of the suffering which the boll weevil had brought into their lives. So, they erected this monument to a bug.

A Ruined Business

When I first started the pastoral ministry in 1983, I spent some significant time with a man who was discipling pastors in the Birmingham, Alabama area. He had been a very wealthy business executive who had lost everything. He had had no inappropriate business practices. He did everything biblically he was supposed to do. For no apparent reason, he was squashed by the marketplace.

When he arose from the ashes of his crash, the Supreme Commander had put him on a new trajectory, a new mission, a new deployment. This man became an incredible discipler of pastors. His ministry to us was worth more than 10 years of seminary tuition. He was supported by a few wealthy business men in Birmingham, and this man was very aware that the Lord had shut him down in business because the Lord was going to use him to bless and to equip me and others like me for the rest of his life.

The last that I heard, he was still at it.

A Quadriplegic

How many of us know the story of Joni Eareckson Tada? At about the same age as Joseph was, Joni's life was turned upside-down. With a simple dive into the water, she became a quadriplegic. Her life would never be the same, and her trajectory was radically altered. But look at the deployment track on which the Supreme Commander of the Universe put her.

I do not know of anyone else in my lifetime who has been as influential for the Kingdom of God in helping us understand suffering as Joni has been. I once was on the same stage as Joni in an assembly of believers – it was a thing of beauty to see the love of Jesus which continues to shine in her face and to hear the words of trust for her

Father which has only grown deeper through her life of suffering.

You know, when Joni speaks on the subject of suffering, everyone takes notice and listens because her "deployment" to quadriplegia has opened up a world of insight for all of us. I really do love her perspective upon suffering which I recently read:

> *For I sure hope I can bring this wheelchair to heaven. Now, I know that's not theologically correct. But I hope to bring it and put it in a little corner of heaven, and then in my new, perfect, glorified body, standing on grateful glorified legs, I'll stand next to my Savior, holding His nail-pierced hands. I'll say, 'Thank you, Jesus,' and He will know that I mean it, because He knows me. He'll recognize me from the fellowship we're now sharing in His sufferings. And I will say, "Jesus, do you see that wheelchair? You were right when You said that in this world we would have trouble, because that thing was a lot of trouble. But the weaker I was in that thing, the harder I leaned on You. And the harder I leaned on You, the stronger I discovered You to be. It never would have happened had You not given me the bruising of the blessing of that wheelchair.*[20]

Some of My Trajectory

In my own life orbit, I have tasted a number of the Warrior King's deployment changes in my life. The Lord called me to leave law school (which I loved immensely) and a promising lucrative career in law. The Lord called me to leave the military (which I loved beyond description) and go into the ministry (which I did not initially think was a good match for me and my personality – but boy, was I wrong about that one!). The Lord called me twice to leave one church and move my ministry and my family and my life to another church and to another location.

Each of those deployment changes were rather painless and did not entail much deep suffering. But, there have been a couple deployment changes that did involve some pretty serious suffering.

First

I have already mentioned in an earlier chapter of the way the Lord changed the trajectory of my family's life when He blessed us with a special handicapped child (Craig Jr.). Without any doubt whatsoever, I can tell you that had Craig not been handicapped, both my wife Jaime and I were on a parenting course destined for disaster.

It was "in the cards" (to use a "fortune-teller" secular expression) for me to become that pushy demanding father who would try to "remake" his children in his own image and to drive them (with whips, if necessary) to athletic and academic 'gold medals'.

Cerebral Palsy changed everything in our parenting paradigm (well, almost everything – I still encouraged my children to set some pretty high moral and academic standards for themselves).

Craig's suffering burned holes into our hearts. To watch your two-year old not be able to walk and to see the other children look at him as if he was from another planet; to see the other kids run off and play and leave him behind as if he was a nobody; to see him attempt to walk on the school grounds only to see him fall in front of his schoolmates – well, I could tell you a thousand stories, but I won't because Craig is going to read this book, and he is probably going to get on my case as it is.

Suffice it to say, that Craig's handicap was used by the Lord to take us into an entirely different "deployment" as parents, a trajectory which would forever change our hearts and minds concerning what it meant to bring up a child in "the discipline and instruction of the Lord." (Eph. 6:4). Jaime and I were changed comprehensively. Our parenting path was altered. Like Robert Frost, we chose a parenting highway which was "less travelled". And that alternate road has made all the difference.

Second

There was one vocational deployment over the years which did entail some heart-break. Like Joseph, I also felt in my heart betrayed by a band of brothers and sold into slavery. I must admit that my understanding of why the Lord allowed it to happen was pretty obscure at the time. It was a great place of ministry and a great body of believers, and the Lord was blessing and growing our fellowship beyond measure. To be candid, I did not see the big picture at first.

However, the picture of the Lord's side of the tapestry has become much clearer as time has passed. The truth is that I would never have taken the path which I took had the events not occurred as they did. I now have to admit that I have not had this much fun doing ministry in twenty years. He has allowed me to fall in love with a church full of mavericks and misfits just like me. I get to write. I get to pastor. I get to preach. I get to have fun with my flock – for me, this may be the best of my ministry years.

Like Joseph, I can say with all sincerity that regardless of their motives for their actions, God meant it for good.

Summary

We have looked so far at two of God's possible purposes for our suffering which do entail examining ourselves for particular sins and opening ourselves up to His conviction which leads to repentance, brokenness, the cross, and His grace.

1. *Deliverance* (of unbelievers)
2. *Discipline* (of believers)

We also have looked at two of God's possible purposes for our suffering which do not seem connected to any particular sin in our lives.

3. *Development* (of believers)
4. *Deployment* (of believers)

For more than 20 years in ministry, I had only these four Ds (or purposes) for suffering. However, when our youngest child, Clete, was killed at the age of 16, the Lord led me to consider an additional understanding of His purposes for suffering as an instrument of sanctification. We have one final purpose to explore as to why the

Warrior King might choose to choreograph suffering into the lives of believers. Like *Development* and *Deployment,* this final purpose (*Destiny*) does not seem to have much connection to any specific sins in our sanctification walk with Him.

CHAPTER EIGHT

The Fifth Purpose for Suffering: Destiny

But God will look to every soul like its first love because He is its first love. Your place in heaven will seem to be made for you and you alone, because you were made for it – made for it stitch by stitch as a glove is made for a hand.[21]
C.S. Lewis

When God issues a call to us, it is always a holy call. The vocation of dying is a sacred vocation. To understand that is one of the most important lessons a Christian can ever learn. When the summons comes, we can respond in many ways. We can become angry, bitter or terrified. But if we see it as a call from God and not a threat from Satan, we are far more prepared to cope with its difficulties.[22]
R.C. Sproul

The final purpose (at least in this "5D" paradigm) for why the Lord might choreograph suffering into the lives of believers is entitled the purpose of *Destiny*. For 25 years, I taught the 4 Ds of suffering to my flocks. However, after we lost our son, Clete, the Lord led me to embrace this fifth purpose for Him taking us through the Valley of the Shadow.

This purpose is fairly simple to describe: the Lord sometimes leads us into the pit of suffering because

He is preparing in us a deeper yearning to go to our eternal home.

As Paul would describe his readiness to go home, he depicted it in these terms (Phil. 1:21-24):

> For to me, to live is Christ, and to die is gain.
> But if I am to live on in the flesh, this will
> mean fruitful labor for me
> And I do not know which to choose.
> But I am hard-pressed from both directions,
> Having the desire to depart and be with
> Christ, for that is very much better;
> Yet to remain on in the flesh is more necessary
> for your sake.

Paul had an open hand, holding life here on earth loosely and not clenching it too tightly. He could see the joy and the blessing of living here on earth glorifying God and enjoying Him now. He could also envision the joy of leaving this life and entering into our eternal joy. *That, my friends, is a beautiful place to be.*

I really must admit that I now believe that it is this posture (I can go or I can stay, either way – blessed be the Name of the Lord) which best positions us to bear the greatest fruit for His Kingdom and to follow Him in the War of Wars with the greatest amount of victory. In this posture, one of Satan's greatest weapons against us, which is fear, is totally ineffective to neutralize our service to our King.

The question is, of course, how does the Lord get us into this posture. Lord, I am yearning for You to take me home to my destiny, but I am also eager and ready to follow You into the battle of your War against the darkness. I am at Your service and serve at Your pleasure. Use me here or take me home. Either way is OK with me as long as I am with You.

How in the world do we ever get to this place? Answer: God gets us to this place by using His instrument of suffering to mature us to this point in our sanctification.

Consider the Suffering of My Friends, Jim and Lois

It was sometime in late summer of 1983 when I met Jim and Lois. They visited the church which I was pastoring for worship one Sunday. They were somewhere in their late fifties or early sixties. Jim was deeply in love with his wife of three or four decades. Lois had Parkinson's disease.

I remember the first covered-dish supper which they attended. Jim was so sweet as he leaned over his wife and cut up her meat for her because her shaking was so intense that she was unable to cut up her own food. I fell in love with these two. Jim eventually became an Elder and a leader of our church.

Maybe better than anyone I have ever seen, Jim found that mysterious balance between holding down an important job (so that he could support his family), ministering to the flock of the church, and loving and caring for his beloved wife. He was one of the best shepherding Elders I have ever known. His evangelistic zeal and willingness to go and visit evangelistically was second to none. His love for Lois was a thing of beauty.

Then, sometime in the second half of the 1990s, Jim was mugged and beaten up by a gang of hoodlums. Even though I was no longer pastor at that church, I called Jim. I was blown away by this man's faith in the Lord and his forgiveness for those young men. When I asked him about his unusual response, he told me that the Lord was just helping him to turn loose of this life a little more easily. The Lord was getting him ready to take him home.

Sometime in the next year or so, Jim was diagnosed with Parkinson's disease. I have never heard of a married couple both having Parkinson's. Lois' decline was slow and gradual, but Jim's decline was much more rapid. Within another year or so, Jim was in worse condition than Lois.

When I next saw them, Lois was driving Jim (I had never seen that before). He was frail and feeble, but his mind was still sharp. As I watched Jim shake almost uncontrollably, I asked him how he was doing. With a smile I will never forget, he said:

> *I am ready to go home to be with Jesus; I do not want to leave Lois, so I am also ready to stay here as long as He wants; I can't do as much physically as I used to be able to do – but I can still pray. Whatever the Lord wants, I am ready.*

Both Jim and Lois now fellowship with the Lord.

As the years seem to keep passing by ever so quickly, I am discovering that more and more of my friends with whom I began ministry are suffering from the aging process. Even without a disease such as Parkinson's or

Alzheimer's or cancer, our bodies begin to break down and fall apart. In time, we all begin to see that our bodies were not intended to be here forever. We are beginning to wind down, and we realize that our destiny lies elsewhere.

The Lord may indeed lead us into the Valley of the Deep Darkness of aging and disease in order to get us ready for our next adventure with Him, *which is our destiny*.

Consider the Suffering of My Friend, Bill

I met my friend Bill more than a decade ago. We both share a great passion for hunting. We were roughly the same age. We liked the same kind of things. We had the same kind of personality (lions!). Even though I was his pastor, we became close friends – a sometimes rare experience for a pastor. We discovered that we were both men with city minds and country spirits.

On a hunting trip in our first year of knowing each other, we were processing a deer for the meat freezer when I noticed an unusual shaking in one of his hands. I mentioned it to him, and he said that it had just started doing that and that he would go and get it checked out.

After several years of doctor's visits, the diagnosis finally came down: This too was Parkinson's.

Much like me, my friend Bill is a passionate man. He is passionate about all aspects of life: he is passionate for his wife, he is passionate for his precious daughter, he is passionate for his hunting, he is passionate for the business which he owns, and he is passionate to be "right" about most things (particularly, when he and I disagree on something). He is just passionate about all of his life.

I have known other friends like Bill, people very intense about life and loving life fully. However, as their lives proceeded, these other folk unfortunately began to hold on way too tightly to the things which they loved in this world. Rather than hold the things of this world loosely and enjoy them under the Sovereign smile of the God Who has blessed them with these blessings, they began to love the gifts more that the Gift-Giver. And when it came time (which it always does) for the Lord to loosen their grips upon the things of this world, these intense and passionate lovers of life became very bitter in their souls.

In some respects, all of us wrestle (to some degree or the other) with this dynamic of letting go of the things of this life. Most of us have to let go of the mirage that one day we will grow up and be Emperor of something. We have to let our children go. Some of us have to say goodbye to our spouses. Most of us usually have to let go of our vocations (it is called retirement, for those who believe in that). We have to let go of our health. We have to give up bladder control, and so on. Indeed, eventually, we have to let go of everything here on this planet. To quote an old adage, "There are no U-Hauls behind the hearse." But, I believe that it is often the most passionate among us who struggle the most to "let go."

I do not know what Bill would have been like at this point in his life had he not contracted his disease. I do not know if Bill would have been like some of my other friends who ultimately became bitter about having to "let go" of things. What I can tell you is that Bill does not seem to have gone into that pit of bitterness.

Bill's disease has progressed slowly over the last ten years. I have watched my friend grapple with his disease with his body, his mind, and his soul. Bill is a fighter – he has fought this disease ferociously at every step. He fights valiantly still today. But, he seems to have faced the reality of the hand which he has been dealt, and he is avoiding the plague of bitterness in this last quarter of his life on earth.

Even more important than avoiding this bitterness which so often is associated with "letting go," it appears to me that Bill has begun to change in his relationship with the Lord. Since I have known Bill, he has always been a believer in Christ and a servant in His Church. In the last few years, however, I have watched Bill's intimacy with Christ deepen in remarkable ways.

I now find my friend much more insightful concerning the spiritual things of life. He is much more vulnerable and transparent about his own sinfulness and his deep need for the Lord to lead him in this life. His prayer life has begun to affect others deeply. His love and his appreciation for those around him has grown tremendously. His zeal for outreach and evangelism has broadened.

While not in any way giving up on his passion for life, Bill seems to value more and more the things which ultimately will "stand the test of time." If God sustains and restores Bill's ability to continue to enjoy his earthly passions, that will be wonderful. But, in my opinion, my friend Bill is more ready now to "let go" of his grip on this life and to look forward to enjoying his destiny with the Lord than if the Father had never lead him into his present suffering.

Consider the Loss of Clete

My son's tombstone reads as follows:

> Clete McAllister Childs
> May 8, 1989-Nov. 18, 2005
> "A godly young man who finished strong for the Lord"
> Jesus – You promised
> I trusted
> Get ready
> I'm coming home!
> John 3:16 | John 14: 1-6

I am Yearning for my Destiny because of Missed Company

Even after many years, it is still impossible to explain to others how much my soul yearns for my son. Of course, I truly love my wife (Jaime), my three living children and their spouses (Craig & Michelle, Laura & James, and Alie), and my grandchildren – Kedron, Trey, Audrey, and Emmaline. But as much as I love them and enjoy them in this life, I still have an ache for Clete.

I am looking forward to hearing his words, "Hey, dad...." I cry as I write, trying to tell you about his hugs. I can't do it. Sorry.

I am pretty certain that it will be Clete whom the Lord will use to explain to me all the answers to the questions in my "gerber jars" where I store all of my difficult questions about life and about God.

There is a poem in our kitchen, and I am sorry, but I do not know its author. I read it as a poem written from Clete to me. Part of the poem reads as follows:

I wanted to tell you how closely I've kept
The memories of you in my heart
And all of the lifetimes that we had to share
Live even though we're apart
But don't cry for me
'Cause I'm finally free

To run with the angels
On streets made of gold
To listen to stories of saints new and old
To worship our Maker
That's where I'll be
When you finally find me

Now don't you be weary cause waiting for you
Are wonders that you've never known
Just hold on to Jesus, reach out for His hands
And one day they'll welcome you home
And that's when you'll be
Finally free, finally free.

I wish you were here, I wish you were here.

My destiny awaits me. My Jesus awaits me. Ultimately, the new earth and the new heaven await me. My body will become new and will join with my soul and my spirit. I will see my son again and get my hug.

I am Yearning for my Destiny because I have Glimpsed the Depths of My Own Soul

This reason for yearning for my destiny is harder to explain. It may be that only some of you will understand me. It may be that only the ones who have a lost a child or a spouse or have experienced some equally catastrophic loss will identify with what I will share here.

As I assess my own personality, I realize that one of my greatest weaknesses as a human being is that I do not let myself feel deeply. I guard my heart somewhat. Over the years, that has hurt some of the folks closest to me who wanted more of my heart and my soul.

The fact is that guarding my heart and soul has deprived me of some of the beauties of feeling deeply. The death of Clete has greatly altered all of that.

This is the part which may be hard to comprehend. In the grieving of the loss of Clete, I hurt and anguished and suffered in parts of my soul which I had no idea even existed. Now by this, I do not mean that I just felt deeply in the normal parts of my soul. No, what I mean is that deep, deep, deep caverns and compartments of my soul opened up that had never let me know they were there.

These caverns in my soul were ravaged by the thunderbolts of grief. They were thirsting for comfort. They were screaming for relief. They burned fiercely and brightly and revealed light-years of depth of soul which I had never tasted. It hurt so bad, and so raw, and so deep that it was only the Holy Spirit who could enter into those caverns and bring healing and comfort.

Then, with an even deeper grace, the Lord slowly closed up those caverns. Only on rare occasions today can I still feel the phantom pain of their existence.

But, now I know that these places exist in my soul. I also seem instinctively to know that when I join my King of Kings in my final destiny that all of these places in my soul will be thrown wide open. It will be in these deep deep chasms where I will feel ecstatic joy instead of grief. I can hardly wait. To feel these magnificent caverns filled up with praise of Him, love of Him, rejoicing with Him. To taste of my Lord in these deep deep places is going to be the greatest of all thrills and passions. For Him to go there – oh, my goodness, *it is beyond my wildest comprehension!*

I know. It sounds like nonsense. I would never have understood it either, if Clete had not died. But he did. And now I know. To be candid, my friends, I await my destiny with a passion.

I am Yearning for my Destiny because Suffering has Tutored me on the Character of my God

One of the biblical benedictions which we use in our community of faith teaches us something about a framework for contemplating the character of our Triune God (2 Cor. 13:14):

> The grace of the Lord Jesus Christ, and
> the love of God, and

the fellowship of the Holy Spirit,
be with you all.

This scriptural benediction contains the framework grid for much of what I have learned about the character of God from the death of my child. Specifically, my sufferings have tutored me about the character of God in three specific arenas:

First, the death of my son has taught me much about the Grace of the Lord Jesus Christ.

The old adage for G-R-A-C-E which I learned as a new believer was “God’s Riches At Christ’s Expense”. Simply stated, Grace meant that God the Son suffered to take my “death” place and pay the price for my sins on the cross that day at Golgotha. Now consider this question: How can I really know what it meant for Jesus to suffer in my stead as my substitute?

- I can read in the Bible all about the flogging posts, the nails, the spear, the cross.
- I can study the commentaries which expound upon the specific process of the crucifixion.
- I can do a medical study of the atrocity of the crucifixion procedure.
- I can watch *Passion of Christ* with all of its visual gore.

But the truth is that the deepest way that I can begin to understand the suffering which my King experienced just for me is to actually experience some of life’s gut-wrenching sufferings myself. I realize that I will never fully comprehend His physical pain on the cross nor His spiritual and emotional suffering as the Father turned His gaze away as the Only Begotten Son drank of the cup of wrath for all of my evil. However, I do believe that losing Clete has given me a much deeper feel for His suffering on my behalf.

I can tell you that the loss of my son produced in my soul a kind of "unrelenting anguish". No matter which way I turned or which way I ran, I was anchored to the pain and anguish – suffering under the unrelenting bondage of my grief and despair. This experience has given me some small insight into my Savior's agony.

When I think of my Savior on the cross, my trauma of the loss of Clete reminds me of His "unrelenting anguish". His was a suffering from which there was no respite. This was His enduring of the just fury of the Righteousness of God. There was nowhere to go and nowhere to hide from the Wrath of the God of the Universe. He chose to anchor Himself to that cross. He chose the shocking agony. He suffered all of that for me. As Augustine has observed, God had one son on earth without sin, but never one without suffering.

Now, after Clete, I understand better the sufferings of His Grace – at least a little.

Second, the death of my son has taught me much about the Love of God the Father.

Like many of you, the truths of John 3:16 were central to my understanding of God's love for me which led to my conversion. If you had asked me then, I would have told you that I understood what it meant when the text said that God so loved me that He gave His Only Begotten Son. The reality is that I did not have a clue.

No one should have to feel what it feels like to lose a child. No one should experience the lightning bolts as they burn your heart inside you. No one! And I will tell you now (knowing what I know now) that I would never *choose* to give up my son – not ever, no way, no how. There is no one whom I love enough to allow my son to be painfully executed in their stead. There is not any person anywhere who is so precious to me that I would take my son's life so that they could live instead.

Yet, the Father *chose* to give His Son to be sacrificed in my place. How could He? Why would He? How can it be that I should gain from this gift of the Father? Is it really possible – is it really true that my Heavenly Father actually loves me that much? I cannot fully grasp this kind of love, but I understand it better now than before.

Third, the death of my son has taught me much about the Fellowship of the Holy Spirit.

I was in my early twenties when I first read Jesus' description of the Holy Spirit in John 14 and 16. He was to be my Comforter. As the years of my walk with the Lord progressed, I felt that comfort sometimes in the normal suffering of life. When my son's handicap struck our home like a hurricane, for the very first time I felt deep ache in deep places – and that is when I really tasted of the Spirit's comfort.

But I spoke earlier of the deep chasms of my soul which were revealed when we lost Clete – when those places screamed out in agony, the Spirit of the Living God jumped into those places with both feet, so to speak. His presence and His fellowship in the deep spots of my inner self was the only balm to bring any kind of healing and encouragement to the roots of my bankrupt self.

I did not actually understand His comfort and His fellowship until I lost my son. Now I understand.

> *The Grace of the Lord Jesus Christ.*
> *The Love of God the Father.*
> *The Fellowship of the Holy Spirit.*

That is my God. There is no one like Him. And I will be with Him forever and ever and ever. *Amen.*

Bring on that Destiny!

Summary of Part II (Some Purposes for Suffering)

We began this Part II of this book with a quote from Charles Spurgeon challenging us to see the "big picture" of our existence--to see beyond the struggles and the sadness of today and to look foward instead and to focus upon the designs of our God Who walks us through the sometimes gloomy streams of our lives toward our ultimate destiny with Him.

As we bring this Part II to an end with this discussion of Destiny, a friend of mine has drawn to my attention certain insights into our Destiny which have been expressed by two great minds, one contemporary and one from years past.

In his important defense of the Christian faith, *Reasons for God*, Tim Keller addresses the problem of suffering by drawing from the climax of the trilogy *The Lord of the Rings*. He observes:

> Sam Gamgee discovers that his friend Gandalf was not dead (as he thought) but alive. He cries, "I thought you were dead! But then I thought I was dead myself! *Is everything sad going to come untrue?*" The answer of Christianity to that question is – yes. Everything sad is going to come untrue and it will somehow be greater for having once been broken and lost.[23]

Keller continues by reminding us that "Embracing the Christian doctrines of the incarnation and Cross brings profound consolation in the face of suffering. The doctrine of the resurrection can instill us with a powerful hope. It promises that we will get the life we most longed for, but it will be an infinitely more glorious world than if there had never been the need for bravery, endurance, sacrifice, or salvation… *This is the ultimate defeat of evil and suffering. It will not only be ended but so radically vanquished that what has happened will only serve to make our future life and joy infinitely greater.*"[24]

Dostoevsky put this another way when he wrote:

> *I believe like a child that suffering will be healed and made up for, that all the humiliating absurdity of human contradictions will*

> *vanish like a pitiful mirage, like the despicable fabrication of the impotent and infinitely small Euclidean mind of the man, that in the world's finale, at the moment of eternal harmony, something so precious will come to pass that it will suffice for all hearts, for the comforting of all resentments, for the atonement of all the crimes of humanity, of all the blood that they've shed; that it will make it not only possible to forgive but to justify all that has happened."* [25]

This future vision of the Hebrew concept of *tikkun olam*, of "things restored to rights," inspires us in our day-to-day battles. It gives us the "long view" of life that helps us to be steadfast, even in the midst of our present sufferings. In this War of Wars, we are well to be reminded that our loving Father chooses:

- sometimes to use the instrument of suffering to *deliver* us from the bondage of darkness
- sometimes to *discipline* us from the power of darkness in our own lives
- sometimes to *develop* us for our role in the War
- sometimes to *deploy* us into battle in that War

And sometimes to prepare us for our ultimate *destiny* when we will war no more.

Let not your heart be troubled; believe in God, believe also in Me. In My Father's house are many dwelling places; if it were not so, I would have told you; for I go to prepare a place for you. And if I go and prepare a place for you, I will come again, and receive you to Myself; that where I am, there you may be also. - John 14: 1-3

PART III

Some Postscripts on Suffering

And David said in his heart,
"I shall now perish one day by the hand of Saul."
1 Samuel 27:1

The thought of David's heart at this time was a *false* thought, because he certainly had no ground for thinking that God's anointing him by Samuel was intended to be left as an empty unmeaning act.

On no one occasion had the Lord deserted His servant; he had been placed in perilous positions very often, but not one instance had occurred in which divine interposition had not delivered him. The trials to which he had been exposed had been varied; they had not assumed one form only, but many – yet in every case He who sent the trial had also graciously ordained a way of escape. David could not put his finger upon any entry in his diary, and say of it, "Here is evidence that the Lord will forsake me," for the entire tenor of his past life proved the very reverse. He should have argued from what God had done for him, that God would be his defender still.

But is it not just in the same way that we doubt God's help? Is it not mistrust without a cause? Have we ever had the shadow of a reason to doubt our Father's goodness? Have not His lovingkindnesses been marvelous? We have had dark nights, but the star of love has shone forth amid the blackness; we have been in stern conflicts, but over our head He has held aloft the shield of our defense. We have gone through many trials, but never to our detriment, always to our advantage; and the conclusion from our past experience is, that He who has been with us in six troubles, will not forsake us in the seventh. What we have known of our faithful God, proves that He will keep us to the end.

Let us not, then, reason contrary to evidence. How can we ever be so ungenerous as to doubt our God? Lord, throw down the Jezebel of our unbelief, and let the dogs devour it.

C. H. Spurgeon

Charles Spurgeon,
Morning by Morning

CHAPTER NINE

A RARE Response to Suffering

Suffering may strip us of all other dignities, but the one dignity which suffering
can never take from us is our choice of
our response to its injustices.
Dr. Viktor Frankl

Naked I came from my mother's womb and
naked I shall return there.
The Lord giveth and the Lord taketh away.
Blessed by the name of the Lord.
Job 1: 21

If you will remember from the end of the chapter on "Important Truths about Suffering," I mentioned that one of the final things that we would consider together in this short book would be our response to suffering. Often when we experience the Valley of the Shadow, there is so much that is beyond our control. However, there is one thing which the Lord has ordained to remain within our ability to influence, and that is our response.

The Story of Viktor Frankl

Many of us have heard the account of the psychologist, Viktor Frankl, who was taken captive, humiliated, tortured, and abused during World War II. In his book, *Man's Search for Meaning,*[26] Dr. Frankl recounts the inhumanity of the Nazi concentration camps and then reflects upon the potential responses which are available to human beings who are experiencing such deep unjust sufferings.

In contrast to other opinions which conclude that human beings caught up in such circumstances of suffering have no real choice but to mentally, emotionally, and spiritually succumb to those circumstances, Dr. Frankl offers an alternative. This is not some academic ivory-tower hypothesis. This is a real alternative asserted by a man who himself endured some of the most horrendous sufferings imaginable.

In the concentration camps, Frankl observed men who made a choice. They made a choice to maintain their human dignity and to rise above their circumstances. They made a choice to own their response to their captors and their torturers. He asserts that there is always a choice – when all else has been stripped away, it is the last of the human freedoms. It is that inner spiritual freedom to choose one's attitude toward one's circumstances of sufferings. It is the choice to own your response.

To summarize Frankl's contention: Suffering may strip us of all other dignities, but the one dignity which suffering can never take from us is our choice of our response to its injustices.

Viktor Frankl claims that he witnessed men who owned their response to their sufferings. I believe him. I believe him because I am convinced that we see such ownership of response in numerous places in the Word of God.

Consider Job

Job 1:1 describes Job as a man who was "...blameless, upright, fearing God, and turning away from evil." And what did he get for his virtues? The Lord dangled Job in front of Satan who did everything he could to devour this blameless man – in body, soul, and spirit.

Broken-hearted in grief after losing all of his children and physically being tormented by itching festering boils all over his body, what did Job say? Better yet, what would you and I say to the Lord God about the Valley of the Shadow which God Himself had allowed? Well, on second thought, maybe we should not contemplate what we might have said, maybe we should simply consider Job's response.

To his "endearing" wife who suggested that Job should just curse God and die, he replied (Job 2:10):

> You speak as one of the foolish women speaks.
> Shall we indeed accept good from God and
> not accept adversity?

To his Lord, King, and Heavenly Father, he said (Job 1:21):

> Naked I came from my mother's womb
> And naked I shall return there.
> The Lord gave and the Lord has taken away.
> Blessed be the name of the Lord.

The one thing that Satan can never steal from us is our response to our Father! Satan lost.

God 1- Satan 0

Consider the Apostles

These down- to-earth everyday folks were just trying to figure out the Gospel. It seemed pretty simple to them. He died (to pay the penalty for our sins). He rose again and was alive (to conquer death and all fear for us). They were supposed to tell others about it. Why should the religious leaders of the day be so upset – after all, He was their Messiah also.

Whatever they were thinking, I cannot help but believe that the flogging posts were not in their best plan for how the day would work out there in Acts 5. The flogging posts were no picnic. They left there with blood pouring out of the mangled mass which used to be their backs. The blood ran down the back of their legs so intensely that everywhere the soles of their feet touched the ground, there was a trail of bloody footprints. The pain and the shock from the loss of blood was overwhelming. What do you suppose they were thinking as they staggered away from those flogging posts?

Where did we go wrong? What did we say which was so wrong? Where was the Holy Spirit as those whips came down tearing up our backs? Why didn't God show up to help us? Why didn't the Lord intervene and stop it? Why didn't…

No, that was not how they viewed the outcome of the day. Rather, their final word on the day was that they were "... *rejoicing that they had been considered worthy to suffer shame for His name.*"

Again, Satan cannot force our response to suffering. Whenever we choose to flee to our Heavenly Father and trust Him and rest in His arms, it does not matter what darkness throws at us, Satan loses. *Every time.*

God 2 - Satan 0.

Consider Stephen

Stephen is described in Act 6 as "*...a man full of faith and of the Holy Spirit...*" and then again as one "*full of grace and power...*" Surely, a man such as this could be valuable to serve in the War of Wars for a long and full lifetime. Surely, this is the kind of man which the Lord God would protect so that he could bear fruit for the Kingdom for decades.

When the flock of the Shepherd confirmed Stephen to be a deacon, I doubt that they had any idea of how short-lived his ministry would be. Now, I have to admit that as I read Stephen's defense of the faith, I realize that Stephen is not a politician. He is not abusive in his speech, but neither does he soft-sell or back-peddle on the matter of the Gospel – and the matter of sin. He speaks the truth in a straightforward manner, without sugar-coating it. *Kind of like Jesus.*

The crowd was "*cut to the quick,*" which means that they flew into a mob-like rage. There was fury in this crowd of religious people (church people can be that way sometimes). This time, however, this witness of Christ is not taken to the flogging posts. Rather, he is pushed and manhandled and taken outside the city and thrown into the stoning pit. There was no doubt what was going to happen.

Satan has moved the ire of the mob to a fever-pitch, and Jesus Christ has allowed it to happen.

Now, the stones begin to fall – not marble-size rocks or even baseball-size stones – no, these are bowling ball-size boulders. They begin to crush Stephen's extremities, then the core of his body causing unbelievable trauma of broken bones and punctured torso. Boulder after boulder pulverizes his frame.

How could the King of Kings allow this? How could Satan be given such free reign over such a godly man as this? As with Job, we might well ask: *Where is Jesus?*

The Word of God tells us exactly where He is. Stephen sees his Savior *standing* at the right hand of God (7:56). You know, we do not normally see the Son of God standing at the right hand of His Father – He is usually sitting. Why is Jesus standing now as Stephen faces his Valley of the Shadow?

There are a lot of commentary explanations, but the one which I like best is the assertion that Jesus is standing because this is an unprecedented historic crossroads event. This is a key and critical moment in the flow of the Gospel to the ends of the earth. Remember, Saul (Paul) is holding the robes of the stoners and cheering them on as they slaughter this man in this pit (7:58; 8:1).

I envision Paul to be smirking and watching for the emotional and spiritual breakdown of Stephen. But instead, Paul sees a face full of the Holy Spirit gazing intently for the Presence of his Lord (7:55). And instead of the normal curses and pleas, Paul heard these words from the lips of Stephen: *"Lord, do not hold this sin against them!"* (7:60).

Paul had probably heard the rumors of almost the same words being spoken by Christ as He looked down on His enemies at the foot of the cross. But, now Paul sees and hears the words with his own eyes and his own ears.

Several commentaries describe it like this (a paraphrase): the mission of the Church expanding to the ends of the earth owes its very existence to the fact that Paul had the face and the last words of Stephen hauntingly and indelibly imprinted upon his heart and his conscience. Even though he tried to purge himself of the portrait of Stephen in his mind by persecuting the Way and extinguishing them from the face of the earth, he could never get the picture of Stephen out of his soul. And then came the road to Damascus, and the House on Straight Street . . . and the rest is world history.

You see, it was Stephen's response to his Valley of the Shadow which the Holy Spirit used to influence Paul and to launch the Great Commission. Satan took his very best shot at shutting down the young seminal Church in Jerusalem. Satan could influence the crowd, and he could influence Paul. But the one thing which Satan could not control was Stephen's response to his experience of suffering.

God 3 - Satan 0.

Synopsis

You and I could continue this study. We could look at additional Old Testament believers and New Testament believers, and we would find a similar pattern:

- In the Master's Sovereign reign over His Church, He choreographs Valley of the Shadow experiences into the lives of believers for a number of different holy purposes.
- Satan attempts to bring the heat and to control everything he can to use the season of suffering as a context to turn the believer against trusting his Heavenly Father and instead drift away from the Lord and thus lose his fruitfulness in the Kingdom of God.
- But, Satan cannot control the response of the believer. The response of the believer is beyond Satan's touch. The response of the believer is our opportunity to trust our Redeemer and to fall into His arms. We can choose our response to suffering!

My Personal Strategy to Respond to Suffering: It's R-A-R-E

I wish that I could tell you that my first response to suffering in my life has always been similar to the response of Viktor Frankl. I wish that I could tell you that I usually am able to trust God's Sovereignty at the very beginning of my seasons of suffering. I wish that I could tell you that my responses to the Valley of the Shadow are like that of Job, Stephen, Jesus, Paul, and the Apostles. Actually, I could tell you all that – *but it would not be true.*

The real truth is that my initial responses to the Lord leading me into the Valley of the Shadow are most often self-focused, self-centered, rebellious, hard-hearted, angry, bitter – generally, not very pretty. However, the Lord has taught me through some very hard lessons over a great number of trials that once I am finished with my initial temper-tantrum and pity-party that I need to repent, then to draw near to Him, and then to follow a pretty simple biblical process which enables me to find my balance in this particular season of suffering.

I will share with you my personal response process. Please do not take this to be some kind of magic formula. It is not the case that if you just follow this formula, you will get some magical result. It is not about some formula. Rather, it is about trusting Him and believing that He will ultimately work out all things for the good for those love Him and are called to His purposes (Rom. 8:28). Nevertheless, this approach has blessed me deeply when I have journeyed in the Valley of the Shadow. I call it R-A-R-E.

R = REJOICE

Nope, it is actually not a typo. I really do believe that the first healthy step in a biblical response to suffering is to *rejoice.* You may not agree with me here, and that is OK. But I am pretty sure that God is on my side. At least, that is the impression which I get when I read the Scriptures. Let us revisit a few of our passages on suffering.

Romans 5: 3-5 describes that process which flows through the tribulation to perseverance to proven character to hope. However, did you notice that first step: "EXULT in our tribulations…"

James 1:2-4 describes that process which flows through various trials to faith-testing to endurance to maturity. However, watch out for that first step: "CONSIDER IT ALL JOY, my brethren, when you encounter various trials…"

1 Peter 1: 6-7 describes that process which flows through various trials to be tested by fire to the imperishable faith to the praise/glory/honor of Jesus. But that first step is a doozy: "In this you GREATLY REJOICE, even though now...you have been distressed by various trials…"

Acts 5: 40-41 depicts the Apostles leaving their flogging events "REJOICING that they had been considered worthy to suffer shame for His name."

What is wrong with all these folks – Paul, James, Peter, the Apostles? Are they delusional? Are they on drugs? Are they a brick shy of a full load? How in the world can someone in their right mind advise us that we should rejoice when we find ourselves in the Valley of the Shadow?

No, they are not deranged. Rather, in their walk with the Warrior King they had learned something that we all will need to learn if we are going to emerge from the Valley of the Shadow healthier than when we entered it.

We are in the Valley because He has ordained it. We are in the struggle because He has decreed it. We are in the trial because He has choreographed it to be so. He has a plan, and it will work out for good for His Children who trust Him. He has not deserted us. He loves us more than we can even dream of being loved. Our Best Friend is running the show, and He knows that this is where we need to be for now.

Once we understand this fact in the deep recesses of our heart, then we can join with the blacksmith whom we discussed earlier. Once we really get it that we, the jars of clay, are in the hands of the Potter and that He is working on us to make something beautiful, then we too can say:

> *Lord, put me into the fire if You will; put me into the water if You think I need it; do anything, You please, O Lord, only don't throw me on the scrap heap.*

Please allow me to illustrate. I remember in high school when as a sophomore, I tried out for the varsity football team. Now, I had played football in both elementary school and Junior High, so I knew what I was signing up for.

- two-a-day practices in the 100 degrees of August in South Alabama

- coaches screaming at me calling me degrading names
- boys a lot bigger than me putting crushing blows upon my head, shoulders, chest – well, just about all of my body
- running sprints until I vomited
- doing leg lifts until ever muscle in my stomach cramped
- lifting weights until neither my legs nor my arms worked properly
- guaranteeing myself six months of cuts, bruises, pulled muscles, injured limbs, etc.

Think about it. What fool would volunteer for this kind of abuse and punishment? You know what I did when they called off my name as making the team? I yelled for joy (you heard me right, with joy!). I got a huge smile on my face. I hugged my friends who also made the team – all kind of responses which looked a lot like JOY!

Why? Because I trusted that when I had run the gauntlet of that rigorous training, the finished product might be a young man who would step out upon the field of battle and have something to contribute to his team.

The truth is that when my life suddenly takes a turn for the Valley of the Shadow and I realize that difficulties or struggles are on the horizon, I actually recall my memories of those "two-a-days" in August. I also remember my basic training in the Army. I bring to my mind the "spiritual two-a-days" which the Lord has led me through.

I intentionally bring to my heart those portraits of my life when I have gone through hard times only to discover that they eventually produced a "product" that was better at the end of the adventure than what it was going into the endeavor.

I love the words of encouragement which John Bunyan has Hopeful speak to Christian in Christian's time of despair:

> *Your anguish does not mean that God has forsaken you; He merely wants to test you to find out whether you will remember how good He has been to you so far and will lean on Him in your present troubles."*[27]

This is when I go crawl up into the arms of my Heavenly Father and have a talk with Him. I tell Him that I love Him, and I know that He loves me. I tell Him that I know that this is going to hurt. I tell Him that I wish it would stop. I tell Him that if this is what He wants for me, then I know that He will make it work out for the best for me.

Then I tell Him that I really do *rejoice* that He loves me enough to *deliver* me, to *discipline* me, to *develop* me, to *deploy* me, and eventually to lead me to my *destiny*. I am excited that He believes that I am a worthwhile project, and that He has chosen to not throw me on the scrap heap. Finally, I tell Him that it is with joy that I look forward to the end result that He is going to bring forth.

You may can find another way to get to joy in the Valley of the Shadow. That is the way I do it.

A = ACTION

One of the more unusual books in the Bible is the book of Esther. It is a quaint account of a snapshot of time in the history of the Old Testament believers. For me, my favorite verse in this book is when Mordecai encourages Queen Esther to explain the plight of the People of God (who were on the brink of extinction) to a fairly unpredictable king who might listen to her or who might take her life. These were Mordecai's words:

And who knows whether you have not attained royalty for such a time as this?

Let me share with you my take-away from this verse. Whenever hard times come, we need to ask ourselves whether or not the Almighty God of the Universe has positioned us in this "pit time" so that we can take an action of some sort which might somehow influence the outcome of the suffering.

Whenever the Lord allows me to see a Valley of the Shadow on the horizon, I will ask myself a handful of questions to help me discern whether or not God is calling me to action in this matter:

Question #1: Authority?

Has the Lord given me any biblical "*authority*" in this matter (in which He has positioned me) which I might utilize to affect the outcome of this pit time?

To illustrate, let's say that my family may be heading for a crash and burn because one of my children has made bad choices which are going to bring pain upon everyone. Yet, the Lord says that Jaime and I are the biblical authorities over that child. God may well be positioning me to be His instrument to reign down upon my child the painful corrective disciplinary measures which are needed for my child to see his need to repent which then paves the way for the Holy Spirit to bring conviction which then leads to better choices by my child which then may eventually lead my child to arise from the ashes of bad choices and thus experience reprieve from the Valley of the Shadow (and all of my family as well).

Maybe I own a business which is about to take a nose-dive because of the bad choices or the bad habits of an untrustworthy employee. God has placed me in a position of authority and directs me to exercise that authority in the context of my business. I may need to act to utilize the authority which He has bestowed upon me to let the employee go so that the business will not go down in flames.

Or maybe, it is just a matter of exercising authority over my own will and my own heart and my own actions and repenting of my sinful choices and returning to my Master's course.

I know this seems like common sense, but I have known way too many folks who allowed themselves to experience the Valley of the Shadow longer than they had to because they did not act and utilize the authority which the Lord had given them to bring about change.

Question #2: Influence?

If the Lord has given me no biblical authority in this Valley of the Shadow, then I ask myself the second question: Has He given me any "*influence*" upon others which I might could use to massage the outcomes of the suffering.

Let's suppose that I have a good friend whose sin or bad choices are taking him down a road to destruction. Suppose this friend likes my friendship and generally listens to my ideas and my advice. Like Queen Esther, I can worry or fret that my friend's response might be angry or hateful, ending our friendship. Like Esther, we may need to hear Mordecai's counsel: maybe the Lord has given us this influence over this friend for just such a time as this and maybe He will use my advice to effect a change in my friend's choices.

Again, I have watched way too many folks sit on the sidelines as couch potatoes and fail to act with their influence and then watch as everything turns to mush. God had placed into their very hands His tool to bring about His desired changed, but they failed to use it.

Question #3: Prayer!

If the Lord has given me no authority and no influence, then the only action which remains open to me is to "*pray*" – when will I pray and for what?

The sum of my advice on this point of ACTION is that we should take any and all actions which God has placed into our quiver of possibilities which might help determine the outcome of the Shadow of the Valley. If we have authority, act. If we have influence, act. If we have neither, then pray. (Of course, we are called to pray even when we have been given authority and/or influence.)

R = RELEASE

Ten years ago when I first met my friend, Bill, who I wrote about in the last chapter, I ran headfirst into what might have been his favorite phrase at that point in time: "*It is what it is.*"

Bill's expression has always reminded of the prayer attributed to Reinhold Niebuhr in 1943:

> *Lord, grant me –*
> *the serenity to accept the things I cannot change,*
> *the courage to change the things I can,*
> *and the wisdom to know the difference.*

It seems to me that when we have accepted and rejoiced about God's Sovereignty over the Valley of the Shadow and we have taken all of the possible actions that God Himself has positioned us to take, then we need to ask our Father to give us the serenity of heart to accept the things we cannot change.

"*It is what it is*" means to me that since our Father is Sovereign and He has not seen fit to change a matter or to give us His instrumentality to act to change the matter or to answer our prayers to change a matter, then we need to let it go. The bottom line at this point is that we have two real choices.

Choice #1: Fear

We can grab this unchangeable dynamic by the handle of *Fear*. What this translates into is that we will continue to anguish over something which God has apparently ordained to be unchangeable (at least for the time being). The name we have for this sin is *worry.*

Choice #2: Faith

We can grab this unchangeable dynamic by the handle of *Faith*. What this translates into is that we release the matter to Him entirely believing that He will bring about the greatest common good for His People, His Kingdom, His War, and us.

Release the entire anguishing matter to the Father Who truly does know best.

We have a prime example for us to follow, do we not?

In the Garden of Gethsemane, Jesus was in an indescribable anguish which you and I cannot even begin to understand. He knew that all of the vials of God's Holy Wrath were about to be poured out upon Him. He knew that becoming sin on our behalf would mean that His pure, righteous, and just Father would have to look away from His only begotten Son. Jesus knew what was going to happen. He entreated His Father – stop it, please.

Can you and I even begin to understand the pain which our Heavenly Father surely must have felt when He heard the plea of His Eternal Only Begotten Son? Can we imagine the excruciating trauma within our Triune Sovereign at this dilemma – let the cup pass from the Son or save the entire Family of God? We may think that we understand the Eternal Decrees, but can we really envision the Holy Father saying "No" to His Beloved Son?

Here is a paradox without any hope of resolution. Now, listen for it! Now come next the words of release:

> Abba, Father! All things are possible for Thee;
> remove this cup from Me;
> *Yet, not My will, but Thy will be done.*

The Holy Son released the outcome and the consequences completely to His Righteous Father. The result is that Satan lost everything. The Holy Son gained everything. And you and I inherited everything.

God everything- Satan 0.

E = Expect

Often in my discipleship groups, I will ask the foundational question: "What is faith?" Almost always, the first student to respond will recite the essence of Hebrews 11:1. While this is a phenomenal Divine definition of faith, I will often refer my students to another Divine definition of faith which is found in Luke 1:45.

In this text, Elizabeth describes the faith of Mary (the mother of Jesus) as follows:

> Blessed is she who believed that there would be a fulfillment of what had been spoken to her by the Lord.

I will often distill for my students this definition of faith as follows:

> Faith is expecting the fulfillment of what God has promised; or
>
> Faith is believing that God will do what He says He will do.

What then should faith lead us to expect in the midst of our experiences of suffering?

It is right here where the "health and wealth" churches lead us so far astray. They say that we should have a faith which expects God to fix the problem, to remove the "thorn of the flesh" (2 Cor 12) which is causing the suffering, and/or to make our world "safe, warm, and comfortable" again. My friends, while I wish it were true, this is not what we should bet the ranch on.

There are, however, at least two promises of the King of Kings and Lord of Lords which we should expect to be fulfilled.

Expectation #1: His Presence

He will be right there in the "Valley of the Shadow" with you. With His Rod and His Staff, the Shepherd promises to walk that lonesome valley with you (Psalm 23:4). As the old rock song goes, "there ain't no mountain high enough and there ain't no valley low enough" to keep Him away from you.

Crawl up in His lap. May all of us who are weary and heavy-laden curl up in His arms and find our rest and our comfort in Him (Matthew 11: 28-30).

Expectation #2: His Good

There is "Good" on the radar scope. Romans 8:28 is very clear on this matter. If you are one of His, God has promised that He will work to cause "all things" (yes, that includes suffering) to work for good for those who love Him and are called according to His purpose.

Friends, I promise you that I have studied the original language (Greek) version of this verse and there are no asterisks or footnotes on this verse which give any exceptions to this promise anywhere, anyhow, anyway. He will make it work out for good for those of us who are His. While we may not always understand it, you can take it to the bank. You can bet the ranch on it! It is a done deal. The quotable Lewis reminds us that this is true even of the worst of our sufferings:

> *They say of some temporal suffering, "No future bliss can make up for it," not knowing that Heaven, once attained, will work backwards and turn even that agony into glory.* [28]

Rejoice | Action | Release | Expect:
a R-A-R-E response to suffering!

CHAPTER 10

The "One Thing" About Suffering

When you shuck it down to the cob, you are at where the rubber meets the road.
Redneck Friends in Alabama

And we know that God causes all things to work together for good to those who love God, to those who are called according to His purpose.
Romans 8:28

During my years of ministry in Alabama, I ran across a ripe ole saying of some of my "country-folk" friends: "*when you shuck it down to the cob.*" The meaning of this idiom was to refer to the core foundational principle which stands alone when all else has been stripped away.

In our discussion of suffering, I wish to end on the "One Thing" which is the core reality concerning our experience of suffering "*when you shuck it down to the cob*". I believe this is the One Thing:

> **God is Sovereign over all suffering and causes even our suffering to work out for good for those who are His. You can choose to trust this sovereignty and to focus upon**

the Savior Who is Master over all the storms of life or you can choose to focus on the storms themselves and be enveloped in a shroud of fear and darkness. Where you choose to focus foreshadows your outcome!

It is not rocket science. Maybe, one final illustration will help us. Matthew records for us in the Holy Scriptures of Peter's attempt to walk on water in Matthew 14. The historical account goes like this.

Jesus tarried at the mountain to pray after feeding the 5,000. The disciples went ahead to cross the water mass (presumably the Sea of Galilee) in a boat. Jesus would come later. On the boat journey, the disciples ran into a fierce storm, as is common on this particular body of water, and the boat was being battered by the waves provoked by the great winds of the storm.

Right in the midst of this horrendous storm, the King of Kings chose to catch up with the disciples in the storm by walking on the water. The entire context of this event is laden with fear. So, when Jesus arrives at the boat encompassed by the storm, He tells them:

Take courage; it is I; do not be afraid.

It is not real clear to me if the disciples are more afraid of the wild storm which they were caught up in or the reality that their Master had just walked to them strolling upon the top of the water. However, in the midst of this great storm, the brash "can-you-believe-that-he-did-that" Peter made his amazing request of the King: "*Lord, if it is You, command me to come to You on the water.*" I do not know what your overall opinion of Peter is, but you have to admit that he had gumption.

Now, notice what happens (Matthew 14: 29-31):

- At the command of Jesus, Peter stepped out of the boat and went "toward Jesus." Peter walked upon the water.
- But then Peter shifted his gaze away from the Master and toward the wind of the storm; Peter became afraid when he gazed at the storm; and the consequence is that Peter began to sink.
- Jesus rescued Peter and rebuked both Peter and all of the disciples for their lack of faith.
- Jesus got in the boat and the storm ceased. (He really is Master of all of our storms!)

I believe that this is where the rubber hits the road for most of us in our Valley of the Shadow "storm" experiences. When we only *glance at the storm* and we choose to focus our *gaze upon the Master*, we will walk on water (so to speak) in the midst of the storm. The suffering will not do us in.

But, when we choose to focus our *gaze upon the storm*, and we only *glance at the Master,* we will sink into fear. I think that this is probably the "holy-of-holies" when it comes to how we respond to our suffering pits. *We must choose where we will focus our gaze.*

Will we choose to focus our gaze upon the Valley of the Shadow (the storms, struggles, hardships, and sufferings) of our lives? Or will we choose to focus our gaze upon the Warrior King Jesus who is the Master over all of the Valley of the Shadow and over all of its storms and has brought these storms into our lives for some 'good reason'?

It is not easy; yet is not rocket science, either.

Storms come and storms go. The Master remains, Sovereign over everything. That gives us hope, and that makes all the difference. As Luther said, "everything that is done in the world is done by hope."[29]

I wish for Him to enable me to "walk on the water," to endure the storms, and to become all that He ordains and calls me to be. I choose to follow Him into the War of all Wars, regardless of where the road goes. What compels me is hope – hope that our Sovereign God is steadfast in His promises.

So may it be with all of us, for all our days, for us and for our children.

About Dr. Craig D. Childs, Sr.

Dr. Childs is a man of the family – deeply in love with his elegant wife, Jaime, of almost four decades (wed in 1973). He is the father of four children: Craig Jr., Laura, Alie, and Clete (his son who was killed in a car accident at the age of sixteen). Pastor Childs is very excited about his children.

The children of Craig and Jaime Childs are all strong and serious followers of Jesus Christ who have left behind them a wake of accomplishments (both spiritual and secular) which include three valedictorians, a plethora of college scholarships, a head majorette, a head cheerleader, a state champion short story writer, speech contest winners, leaders on the athletic fields, and Kingdom character leaders in youth groups, college ministries, and local church endeavors.

He is also the proud grandfather of four grandchildren: Kedron, Trey (Craig III), Audrey, and Emmaline.

Craig has been in the ministry for thirty plus years and has served as the Senior Pastor of four churches in Alabama and North Carolina. Now in his semi-retirement, he presently serves as the pastor of a new church plant called The Kirk, in Greensboro, North Carolina, and is the founder of The Kirk Institute. His doctoral dissertation

(1983) was written on biblical parental discipline of the preschool child.

Pastor Childs is a man of many passions: a competitive athlete in his younger days (the wrestling mat, the baseball diamond, the football field, the basketball court), an avid fly-fisherman, an accomplished bow hunter, a fervent fan of University of Alabama football, and a delighter in world travel. In a less sensible season of life, this ex-Army Infantry Officer once wrestled two live bears.

Most of all, he is a passionate lover of his Warrior King, Jesus Christ.

About The Kirk Institute

Our Organization

The Kirk Institute is a 501(c)3, non-profit ministry, administered as a charitable fund of United Charitable Programs. It is directed by Dr. Craig D. Childs, Sr, its founder and Program Manager, with oversight from a local and national Board of Advisors.

Our Mission

The Kirk Institute exists because, as the Scriptures teach, there is a spiritual war raging between Christ (along with His followers) and the spiritual forces of darkness. Our mission is to follow the Warrior King in driving back the influence of darkness in our hearts, our homes, our churches, our workplaces, our communities, our culture, our country, and our world. Our specific task at the Kirk Institute is to better equip the Kirk Universal and the broader Christian community to engage in this war against the darkness and to experience Christ's victory in our living both as families and as churches.

Our Services

The Kirk Institute seeks to provide support for biblical, evangelical and Christ-centered communities of faith which are working to renew their commitment to teaching the first principles of the historic Christian faith at every level of development through conversation, teaching, and mentoring. Our services center upon the provision of teaching resources and materials, seminars, leadership training clinics, workshops, retreats, and conferences focused upon equipping each of us to become more effective in the Kingdom War.

Our Website

www.kirkinstitute.org

Our Books

Because of its 501(c)3 status, the Kirk Institute does not sell the books authored by Dr. Childs. Instead, his books may be purchased from the Kirk Warriors, LLC. The Kirk Warriors website dedicated to selling these books is: www.kirkwarriors.org.

End Notes

Introduction

[1] John Piper and Justin Taylor, *Suffering and the Sovereignty of God* (Wheaton, Illinois: Crossway Books, 2006), p. 175.

[2] R.C. Sproul, *Surprised by Suffering* (Wheaton, Illinois: Tyndale House Publishing, Inc, 1989), p.55.

Chapter One: My Familiarity with Suffering

[3] John Piper and Justin Taylor, *Suffering and the Sovereignty of God*, p. 112.

Chapter Two: Lessons Learned from our Suffering

[4] C.S. Lewis, *The Problem of Pain* (USA: Macmillan Paperbacks, 1962), p. 40.

Chapter Three: Important Truths About Suffering

[5] C.S. Lewis, *The Problem of Pain*, p.26.

[6] C.S. Lewis, *A Grief Observed* (New York: Bantam Books, 1961), p. 35. This term Cosmic Sadist is a term utilized by Lewis (in the depths of his initial pain of grief over the death of his wife) to consider the theological possibility that God might be a "bad God."

[7] C.S. Lewis, *The Problem of Pain*, p. 80.

[8] Peter Kreeft, *Making Sense Out Of Suffering* (Ann Arbor, Michigan: Servant Books, 1986), p. 161.

[9] Peter Kreeft, *Making Sense Out Of Suffering*, p.176.

[10] John Piper and Justin Taylor, *Suffering and the Sovereignty of God*, pp. 41, 47.

[11] "Apologetics315.com, "Sunday Quote: Ravi Zacharias on the problem of Evil." *Apologetics 315* online, 14 June 2009 <http://www.apologetics315.com/2009/06/sunday-quote-ravi-zacharias-on-problem.html>.

[12] John Bunyan and Jean Watson, *The Pilgrim's Progress* (in Modern English) (Grand Rapids, Michigan: Zondervan Publishing House, 1978), pp. 16-17.

Chapter Four: The First Purpose for Suffering – Deliverance

[13] C.S. Lewis, *The Problem of Pain*, p.93.

Chapter Five: The Second Purpose for Suffering – Discipline

[14] C.S. Lewis, *The Screwtape Letters*, (New York: HarperCollins Publishers, 2001), pp. 37ff. "*The Screwtape Letters*" was first copyrighted by C.S. Lewis Pte, Ltd, in 1942.

Chapter Six: The Third Purpose for Suffering – Development

[15] C.S. Lewis, *The Problem of Pain*, p. 48.

[16] William F. Arndt and F. Wilbur Gingrich, *A Greek-English Lexicon of the New Testament and Other Early Christian Literature*, (Chicago: The University of Chicago Press, 1957), p. 362.

[17] William F. Arndt and F. Wilbur Gingrich, *A Greek-English Lexicon*, p. 646.

[18] Peter Kreeft, *Making Sense Out of Suffering*, p.142.

[19] ThinkExist.com Quotations. "John Calvin quotes." *ThinkExist.com Quotations Online* 1 April 2012. 30 May 2012 http://en.thinkexist.com/quotes/john_calvin/.

Chapter Seven: The Fourth Purpose for Suffering – Deployment

[20] John Piper and Justin Taylor, *Suffering and the Sovereignty of God*, p. 203.

Chapter Eight: The Fifth Purpose for Suffering -- Destiny

[21] C.S. Lewis, *The Problem of Pain*, pp.147-148.

[22] R.C. Sproul, *Surprised by Suffering*, p. 19.

[23] Timothy J. Keller, *The Reason for God: Belief in an Age of Skepticism* (New York: Riverhead, 2009), p. 33.

[24] Timothy J. Keller, *The Reason for God*, p. 34.

[25] Fyodor Dostoevsky, *The Brothers Karamazov*, Chapter 34, quoted in Timothy J. Keller, *The Reason for God*, p. 33.

Chapter Nine: A RARE Response to Suffering

[26] Viktor Frankl, *Man's Search for Meaning: Introductionto Lego Therapy*, (Boston: Beacon Press, 1962).

Author's Note: I would like for my readers to know that although I have been impressed with Dr. Frankl's reported insights into a human being's ability to own his/her responses to suffering, I have never read any of Dr. Frankl's writings on psychology. Thus, my quotation of Dr. Frankl on this one point should not be construed as any kind of affirmation of either his teachings or his world-and-life-view. CDC

[27] John Bunyan/Jean Watson, *The Pilgrim's Progress* (in Modern English), p. 132.
[28] C.S. Lewis, *The Great Divorce* (Macmillan, 1946), p. 64.

Chapter Ten: The "One Thing" About Suffering
[29] ThinkExist.com Quotations. "Martin Luther quotes." *ThinkExist.com Quotations Online* 1 April 2012. 30 May 2012 <http://en.thinkexist.com/quotes/martin_luther/>.

The Life^n Books Collection
consists of short, topical readers
about the making of a well-lived life.

(Created for people who seek
a life of uncommon yield.)

Other Life^n Readers

ON PEACE:
A Peace of My Mind
By Stuart Briscoe

ON CULTURE-MAKING:
The Manhattan Declaration
Foreword by Charles Colson,
with Study Guide and Commentary

ON SECURITY:
SECURE
By Rick Dunham

www.life-n.com